ESSAYS ON EDUCATORS

Unwin Education Books

Essays on Educators

R. S. PETERS
Professor of Philosophy of Education, Institute of Education, University of London

London
GEORGE ALLEN & UNWIN
Boston   Sydney

First published in 1981

GEORGE ALLEN & UNWIN LTD
40 Museum Street, London WC1A 1LU

© George Allen & Unwin (Publishers) Ltd, 1981

British Library Cataloguing in Publication Data

Peters, Richard Stanley
    Essays on educators.
    1. Education
    I. Title
    370'.8   80-41624

    ISBN 0-04-370103-5
    ISBN 0-04-370104-3 Pbk

Set in 10 on 11 point Times by Inforum Ltd, Portsmouth
and printed in Great Britain by Billings and Sons Ltd.,
Guildford, London and Worcester.

Contents

Preface

This is not the traditional type of book on the Great Educators in which figures like Aristotle, Locke, Comenius and Pestalozzi are dealt with historically and with a wealth of scholarship about their life, times and intellectual antecedents. It is a short collection put together partly from essays that the author has already published and partly from essays written specially for the volume. The essays are concerned with certain themes in the writings of a selected group of educators and make no claim to exhaustive coverage of their thought.

The first group of essays revolves round the respective roles of the individual and society and the place of reason in education. Plato's great work on civic education starts off the collection and the essay is slanted towards his account of the development of reason. In the second, Rousseau's extremely individualistic *Emile* is treated in a way which may surprise some of his progressive followers. The tutor just as much as the child is represented as being very much in the middle of the stage and, in preparing Emile to live with integrity in a corrupt society, the similarity of the tutor to the General Will of the *Social Contract,* which was written at about the same time, is stressed. The defensive individualistic education of Emile contrasts starkly with the preparation of the guardians for citizenship in *The Republic.* The third essay has a double function. First, it tries to restate succinctly the author's revised conception of education and its aims, to acquaint those interested that he no longer holds the views, with which he is still credited, which he put forward in *Ethics and Education* in 1966. Secondly, it is meant to be the democrat's answer to Plato, sketching how it is democracy.rather than aristocracy that institutionalises the use of reason and provides appropriate educational aims. So there is a sense in which the third essay begins where the first one leaves off.

The second group of essays is on the theme of progressivism and tradition. There is a critique of Herbert Spencer's *Essays on Education* which are little known. In the light of modern controversies about the curriculum and the place of science, most attention is given to his essay 'What knowledge is of most worth?'. His elegant and orderly exposition of the 'natural education' of Rousseau and Pestalozzi is also discussed. This is followed by a constructive critique of John Dewey's philosophy of education – the most balanced and powerful statement of the progressive standpoint. The group ends with an essay on Michael Oakeshott, the most subtle, articulate and persuasive of modern traditionalists.

In the third group of essays the author tries to do what he has often said that others should do (for example, in 'Education as an academic discipline' in *Education and the Education of Teachers* (Routledge & Kegan Paul, London, 1977), namely, tackle educational problems from an interdisciplinary standpoint. The first essay is a critique, from a philosophical and psychological point of view, of Kohlberg's theory of moral development – a theory which is very influential in this area. In the second essay there is a critique of motivational theories that are very influential in education, such as those of Skinner, Piaget and McClelland. It is argued that there has been too much concentration on inner drives and mechanical responses and too little attention paid to social and situational factors and the reasons which the agent sees as significant to his actions. Some sociology is introduced into this essay as well as psychology and philosophy.

In brief the book is not just an exposition of the thought of educators. Their writings are used selectively to discuss problems of permanent educational interest and importance.

R S PETERS
University of London Institute of Education

Acknowledgements

The author wishes gratefully to acknowledge permission to reprint the following articles:

'Was Plato nearly right about education?', *Didaskalos*, vol. 5, no. 1 (1975).
'Democratic values and educational aims', *Teachers College Record*, vol. 80, no. 3 (February 1979).
'John Dewey's philosophy of education', in R.S. Peters (ed), *John Dewey Reconsidered* (London: Routledge & Kegan Paul, 1977).
'Michael Oakeshott's philosophy of education', in P. King and B.C. Parekh, (eds) *Politics and Experience* (Cambridge: Cambridge University Press, 1968).
'The place of Kohlberg's theory in moral education', *Journal of Moral Education*, vol. 7, no. 3 (1978).
'Motivation and education', *Paidagogik*, vol. 8, no. 2 (1978) (Gjellerup; in Danish).

Thanks are also due to my colleagues Pat White and Terence Moore for reading and commenting on Chapter 2 and to Terence Moore for reading and commenting on Chapter 4

Part One
The Individual and Society

Chapter 1

Was Plato Nearly Right about Education?

Rousseau claimed that Plato's *Republic* was the best treatise on civic education ever written. Plato was concerned with the development of citizens rather than of individuals. Indeed for him the distinction was more or less meaningless. As is well known he postulated an ideal state divided into rulers, warriors and producers. Justice would emerge if each class did its own job and worked for the common good. His educational system concentrated on the development of a suitably prepared ruling class.

I do not propose to discuss in any detail the wider political aspects of Plato's proposals. Countless volumes have already been written on the subject. Rather I propose to construct a positive critique which will concentrate on one or two educational themes.

In order to indicate the thrust of the title and of this essay I will tell a story, which, I hope, will not shock too many sensibilities. There was a man who went to a marriage bureau to meet the secretary who was trying to fix him up. After a bit of a discussion the secretary said 'Oh, I've got just the girl for you in my file. She comes from a similar background, and is about the same age, and height; her interests are very similar too. There's just one thing about her, though, which might make you pause – she's just a teeny weeny little bit pregnant!' That is really what I feel about Plato. There is just one little thing, which is a bit daunting, if its implications are examined.

To develop this theme I propose to divide this chapter into three main sections. First of all, I shall give an exposition of Plato's proposals about education in some sort of logical order; for one of the most fascinating things about Plato's educational proposals is their logical structure. Secondly, I shall do what it seems to be important to do with any philosopher, namely, to state where I think he was right. Then, thirdly, I shall pass to the little point which seems to me, in its implications, to constitute a major objection to the whole brilliant conception.

In expounding Plato, there is, of course, the problem of historical relativism. By that I do not mean just the details, such as whether children went to school or not, but the whole problem of interpreting in our conceptual system what some of his major notions meant to him, for example, 'reason', 'order', 'justice'. This presents problems if one gets down to such concepts in detail. Nevertheless, I am going to assume that many of his major ideas can be understood by us, more or less, in the same sort of way as he understood them, but I know this is a questionable assumption. What I want to argue is that Plato was right in seeing education to be centrally concerned with the development of reason and that, in the main, he had a very acceptable conception of reason – but there is just one major aspect of his conception of reason which is absolutely non-acceptable. That is going to prove to be the crucial objection to his system.

(1) THE LOGICAL STRUCTURE OF PLATO'S EDUCATIONAL PROPOSALS

Let us look, first of all, at the structure of Plato's educational proposals. What is so attractive about them is their lack of arbitrariness. They follow, quite logically, from a combination of value-judgements and assumptions about human nature. In this way they are exemplary in structure because he had a worked-out theory of knowledge, a worked-out ethical theory and a worked-out theory of human nature. No educational theory can be viable without having these three major components, because, in my view, education is concerned with the development of states of mind involving understanding and knowledge, which are thought valuable, and which have to be attained by processes of learning, which are linked with a view of human nature, and how it develops.

(a) Value-judgements

Let us first of all, then, consider the value-judgements which underlie Plato's whole system. They are one of two types. One relates to the individual, and the other to the political system and the role of the individual in it. In relation to the individual he maintained quite uncompromisingly that the life of reason is the best life possible. This was to be understood in three ways: first of all, he meant by this that the theoretical life (and this meant for him the study of philosophy, mathematics and harmonics) was the best sort of life. This bore witness to the Pythagorean influence on Plato. By coming to understand the underlying structure of the world in such studies the soul becomes one with the Forms. The mind begins to mirror or represent in itself reality, which has a kind of purging influence on the soul.

Secondly, there was the more practical aspect of reason, Socrates' 'care of the soul' which was later developed by Aristotle more explicitly. This was exhibited in self-knowledge and self-control. Thirdly, supporting both aspects of reason, both theoretical and practical, was his account of Eros, of desire. The contrast between reason and passion, in Plato's view, was absurd. He distinguished levels of passion: there was a level of passion which accompanied the life of reason which was distinct from that accompanying the life of the political man, of the warrior, and so on. In other words the use of reason is a passionate business whether you are in pursuit of the Forms or whether you are developing some kind of order in yourself.

These, then, were the basic valuative assumptions about the best life for the individual. Secondly, there were his valuative assumptions about the state, which are more familiar, and which are to be understood, I think, in terms of the rise of professionalism at the time, represented by Isocrates and others, and evident in the dislike of people like Plato and Isocrates for the 'happy versatility' of Pericles' funeral speech. Plato had a supreme contempt for the amateur. He thought that any art has an underlying theory and that anyone who is a professional understands the theory and knows how to apply it. That was one background influence. Secondly, there was the purely historical contingency of the divorce of knowledge from power since the death of Pericles and the rise of demagogues like Cleon. Thirdly, as the Peloponnesian War progressed, there was the upsurge of self-seeking individualism exemplified in the Melian Expedition and, above all, in Plato's mind, in the career of Alcibiades, which seemed to him to personify these sorts of tendencies. And finally, accompanying this, as exhibited in the works of Euripides especially, was the subjectivism, and scepticism, of the young.

Now, given this sort of background, Plato's uncompromising view was that ruling is a professional business and that there should be in the ruler a combination of authority and wisdom; that the wise should rule, and that the best state is the state ruled by those who are the best men. These are the men who, in their own souls, display a passion for reason and understanding, and who are able to apply this to their own behaviour and conduct.

I have no intention of going over Plato's arguments for these value-judgements, which have been heavily criticised by people like Popper and Crossman. At least they are interesting. Whether they are valid is another question. All I have done is to make explicit what his value-judgements are and to put them into some kind of context. I am leaving on one side the question of the validity of his attempt to justify them. So, given these value-judgements about the type of men that are best, the problem of education is to produce people in whom reason is properly developed, who care about the objects of the theoretical life, who are not side-tracked by subjectivism, who know fully what they want, and who have the strength of character to carry it through. If you like, Plato's ideal was a combination of the Spartan and Athenian virtues.

(*b*) *Assumptions about human nature*

Given these value-judgements, if you are going to have an educational system, there is the problem of bringing these people into being. So certain assumptions have to be made about human nature. In Plato these assumptions can be divided into three types. First of all, there is the assumption about the raw material with which the teacher has to work. Plato, I think, was the first systematic environmentalist; he thought that human nature is more or less infinitely malleable. For him Alcibiades was the lesson for all time. Here was a man born with a certain potential, obviously of very high intelligence; but because of his early upbringing even Socrates could do little with him when he became an adolescent. A pattern had been set in his childhood which was almost irreversible. I think that Plato was also what is often now called a perfectabilist, in that he thought that if you can get men in their early childhood, then, given their potential, and given the correct form of social influences, you can produce people like Gandhi or Sir Stafford Cripps or whatever might be the modern parallel for a philosopher-king. It is a matter of the sort of training which you give them. That was his first assumption about the raw material with which the educator is working.

The second one, of course, was that this human potential is unevenly distributed – something that people seem to get very hot under the collar about nowadays in the Jensen controversy. Plato was particularly interested in the differences between people in regard to their intelligence and their social sense – their capacity to co-operate for the common good. He thought that there were marked differences in these particular potentialities. So much then for Plato's assumptions about the raw material with which the educator is working.

The second sorts of assumption are about stages of development. They are now very familiar to us because of the work of Piaget, much of which was anticipated by Plato; for if you look at Plato's account of the stages of development, they are very Piagetian. First of all there is the Freudian level in which Piaget is not much interested. Freud argued that a small infant does not make the distinction between true and false. He has no concept of cause and effect; he does not understand the world in terms of material objects. In other words, he has not grasped the categories which enable us to distinguish what is imaginary. Plato said just this, that the small child lives in what he called the stage of Eikasia, a sort of guess-work or conjecture; he has not got a reality principle or conception of objects of causality. He then gets to the stage of what Plato called Pistis which Piaget calls concrete operations. The world now consists of hard, solid objects which have palpable properties which can be perceived through the various senses. Then, finally, there is the stage of formal operations which actually Plato divided into two. He distinguished within formal operations between Dianoia and Noesís; between the grasp of particular forms, and the kind of synoptic vision of how they all fit together, and how particular forms can be linked with the Supreme Form, the Form of the Good. Now, as we know, these stages of development in Plato were not worked out by sitting children down and asking them questions. There is a sense in which we know it already; for the stages of development form some kind of logical progression. The problem is to make it explicit and to convince people that what is manifestly true *is* true. Piaget, in my view, does it by doing what are meant to be experiments but which manifestly are not. Plato did it by telling stories about the Line and Cave, which are a very graphic or dramatic way of making just these points about cognitive development.

Thirdly, under his assumptions about human nature, come the ways in which people can be influenced in their development. And I think he has at least four suggestions here as to what is important in the way of special influences. First of all, there is the crucial role or what we now call identification or imitation; hence Plato's concern about the example of heroes and the stories of the gods which were to be found in Homer, and his insistence on censorship. The example of teachers is also crucial. Secondly, there is the *indirect* influence of the environment, the influence of beautiful places and beautiful objects on the individual. Thirdly, he draws attention to the importance of play in learning. He talks very strongly about both the indignity and the inefficiency of compelling children to learn things that they do not want to know at that stage. (He says this particularly in the context of learning mathematics.) If children can learn things in a context where they enjoy doing what they are learning, especially while at play, then they are more likely to learn it. Finally, at the stage of reason proper, there is the importance of question and answer, of dialectic as a method of learning.

(c) Consequent educational proposals

So much, then, for the assumptions about human nature. His educational proposals were generated by putting together the value-judgements about the type of individuals to be produced with these assumptions about human nature. Whatever is done in education, for Plato, is a way either of developing in the individual the understanding and love of principles, and the passion for order and symmetry, or of helping the individual to use his reason to impose some harmony on his desires. This is the 'integration of the personality', or whatever you want to call it in modern jargon. In Plato's view gradually the order without is reflected in the order within the individual self. This was a notion which was used in a much more mystical way by Froebel in his writings.

How, then, is this aim of education to be achieved? The guiding rule is that the way in which children are made sensitive to the order in the world, and hence to reproduce this in their own soul, must be appropriate to the stage at which they are. All Plato's educational proposals were therefore designed to sensitise individuals to form and order in the way which is practicable at the stage at which they are. So a start is to be made with the stories of gods and heroes, because at the early stage of Eikasia, when children cannot distinguish between what is real and imaginary, it does not matter whether they are told about heroes or gods or real people; it is the exemplars which matter. What *must* be done is to represent goodness as it is – its unchangeability, for instance. The gods must not be represented as changing or deceiving people – Zeus changing himself into a bull or anything like that. This is all very disgraceful and gives children the wrong sort of picture of what an ideal person is. And because of that, of course, he did suggest a fairly rigid censorship of the sort of stories told to young children.

When the next stage is reached the appeal is through sensory experience and concrete operations, in crafts, and manipulation of materials. Through training the eye and the touch, the individual is sensitised to the beauty of the world, and to its symmetry through his senses. Then, when emotions begin to develop in adolescence, the way in which order gets instilled is through music – good, strong Dorian music with a strong beat and a sense of order – no effeminate trills on flutes or anything like that – something with a really good rhythm to get the order, as it were, beaten into the soul. There is then gymnastics and military service to complete the training of the body and to develop courage – again the emphasis on order. And finally, reason, which has now developed, is ready for specific treatment. The main thing, in the development of reason, is to get people to understand the principles underlying the world (in Plato's terms the Forms), to get them to concentrate on the One in the Many instead of being misled by subjective appearances and perceptual impressions of an individual kind. This is to be done by concentrating them on maths and astronomy, which will give them a proper grasp of principles, of the One in the Many; for these studies provide the key to Reality. Ten years of such study should purge students of subjectivity. It will avoid too much irresponsible criticising in late adolescence before they have the first understanding of what they are meant to be criticising. Then, after this period of settling them down to understand principles, they are ready for the dialectic proper for five years. Finally, after fifteen years' administration, hopefully, they will as it were retire to the Council of Elders and, if they are lucky, they will have a vision of the Form of the Good.

This whole process Plato described as 'turning the eye of the soul outwards towards the light'. By these various methods, starting first of all with the senses, then with the emotions and finally with more intellectual abilities, he hoped to get the individual sensitive to the Forms and to the harmony which unites the Forms, namely, the Good. This, as I said, was an attempt to combine what he considered to be best in Athenian and Spartan education – the inquisitiveness, the theoretical grasp, the sensitivity of the Athenian, with the courage, discipline and order of the Spartan. A combination of what is best in these two, Plato thought, would constitute the ideal man.

(2) PLATO'S POSITIVE CONTRIBUTION

So much then by way of exposition. Now what about where Plato was right? First of all, I would agree with Plato that values are objective – they are not just private preferences – and that education almost by definition must be concerned with the development of valuable states of mind. There is some kind of a contradiction in what I call the specific sense of 'education'[1] – in saying that a person is educated and that this is very regrettable – something bad has happened to him. Secondly, he thinks that education is concerned with a particular segment of what we take to be valuable in that it involves the development of understanding, and hence of reason. There are two aspects of this in Plato: first of all there are what we might call the distinct disciplines or forms of understanding and the development of arts and habits within them, in order words, things like mathematics, morals, aesthetic appreciation, which are, as it were, the channels through which reason flows, and within these there are certain abilities which can be displayed, like judgement and imagination, which have generic properties which go across the different forms of understanding, but which are or can be exhibited in all of them. So that would be the first way in which one understands the development of reason, namely, the development of the different forms of understanding. Plato was particularly concerned with mathematics and morals; he had a pretty strong contempt for what we would now call physical science. He thought that actually to go and look at the world was a ridiculous way to understand it. So he did not go very far in differentiating forms of understanding.

There is also a second way of understanding the development of reason which is related to what might be called a basic level of mental health, which is to be understood in terms of minimum conditions of rationality. This is what Plato was concerned with when he talked about 'the harmony of the soul'. In other words, given that we have desires, unless we are going to be at war within ourselves, in a state of perpetual conflict and frustration, we have to schedule them in a certain way and impose some sort of order on them. Similarly, in regard to our perception of the world, we must have some kind of realism. Being hallucinated would, for example, indicate a lack of development of reason. We have similarly to be able to plan, to control, to take means to ends. All these very obvious things are connected with the elementary development of reason which is constitutive of a basic level of mental health. I think this can be made explicit by developing the sort of thing that Plato says about the harmony of the soul. It involves holding beliefs that are not manifestly mistaken about the ordinary world; being able to plan, to take means to ends, to control one's desires, to impose some sort of order on one's preferences, and so on. In this I am broadly in agreement with Plato.

Thirdly, I agree with Plato that reason and passion are inseparable and that in education what might be called the rational passions are very important. By that I mean that, if one is seriously concerned with developing people in respect of knowledge and understanding, it is not sufficient just to stuff their heads with information. They have to develop a grasp of principles or an understanding of the Forms, but also their interest has to be awakened so that they really care, so that they have this passion for getting to the bottom of things, for getting to the explanation of what Whitehead calls 'the Forms behind the Facts'. And Whitehead regarded all philosophy as a footnote to Plato!

Now, given this positive passion to get to the bottom of things, which was manifest *par excellence* in Socrates, who held that the unexamined life is not worth living, which presupposes a constant striving for clarity and understanding – there are certain passions of a negative sort, which are the obverse side of this – a hatred of irrelevance, a loathing of arbitrariness, a feeling of horror if one is not clear about something. Inconsistency is intolerable and inaccuracy a vice. There are, in other words, certain intellectual virtues and vices which seem to me absolutely central to education and far too little insisted on nowadays. That is one of the things, perhaps, that a more old-fashioned classics education at least used to do for us. I am not quite sure what goes on nowadays but I once went to a classics lesson in America and the insistence was that the students should enjoy it! They were doing, I think, a piece from Seneca about a dolphin. The teacher introduced the lesson by referring to an American baseball team called The Dolphins to get them interested. Then they rattled through the piece, each taking a turn, and reading the Latin in a way which made absolute gibberish of it in good rollicking style. One or two of them had a go at translating the passage. The teacher never bothered to correct them if it was obviously wrong, so I said to her afterwards, 'Why on earth didn't you tell them that this was wrong?' and she said 'Oh you must not do that; they must be happy; they must enjoy it; they must not feel rejected.' I do not suggest for a moment that such practices are widespread; but there are parts of the world where classics is taught in that way. The business of actually getting the thing right is not stressed. Well, I think this shows a cavalier disregard for one of the many intellectual virtues that are central to education.

Then in Plato there is the love of order which is central in Piaget's account also, in which the driving force of intellectual development is equilibration, the balance between assimilation and accommodation. This is a biological metaphor for consistency; Freud, too, said that the desire for order is the basis of civilisation. So there are modern parallels for the passion for order which, for Plato, underlies the whole educational system.

Finally, there is another very fruitful thought in Plato, that I think very important, which was later rediscovered as one of the latest things in sociology by G.H. Mead, namely, the link between individual development and social life. Plato said that thinking is the soul's dialogue with itself and that, when the individual is thinking, what he is doing is taking into his own head a situation in which objections are put, and other points of view are represented. What we understand by 'reason' is not just a kind of gadget that we switch on in our own heads; it consists in representing, as it were, on the private screen of our own minds, a public performance in which we have taken part. It is an internalisation of a form of social life. This is, I think, the very important imaginative thought that runs through Plato's whole account of the link between the development of the individual and the sort of social life in which he takes part. Plato argued, for instance, that the democratic man flourishes in a certain kind of state; the soul of the individual is mirrored in this type of social organisation. The kind of social control to which a person is subjected is very influential with regard to the development of reason. Here again there is a lot of modern sociological evidence to support him. The development of reason seems to be much affected by methods of child-rearing, for instance. If there are arbitrary methods of child-rearing, without explanation, without pointing out the consequences of action, there tends to be a stunting of the development of reason.

(3) CRITICISM OF PLATO

So much, then, for Plato's positive contribution. It sounds from all this as if I am in fundamental agreement with Plato. So why, then, the hesitation? What is the negative point which corresponds to the bit about the girl being pregnant in my opening story? There is no need to fuss about minor or derivative points, for instance, that Plato was wrong about the distribution of human abilities, that he believed that basically most men were moronic, and that only very few were capable of understanding matters of government. That claim might be refuted by appealing to a normal distribution curve of human abilities. Similarly there is no need to press the objections to 'noble lies' and censorship. Anyway that raises very complicated matters; for Plato had a sophisticated view of truth-telling, the role of myths, and being in a state of truth or error.

My major objection to Plato is that, although I agree with him that education is centrally concerned with the development of reason, his conception of reason is in the end indefensible. He believed that its development culminates in certainty of the sort that he found in geometry. Geometry fascinated him; this seemed to him the most amazing feature of the human mind, that human beings could, as it were, just sit and work out abstract formal systems, as the Pythagoreans did, and that these provide the basic understanding of the structure of the world. And this was *certain*; there was no room for normal human bias and fallibility in geometry. Plato thought that all reason was like this, not only in mathematics but also in morals. In morals he thought it possible for a few to have this sort of understanding of the Form of the Good. This provided the philosopher-kings with a similar kind of certainty. And if Plato was right, if in the end morality depended on the vision of the wise and there was some kind of certainty about moral issues, I think both his view of education and his political system would be very difficult to reject. But I think that this view is mistaken. It is a mistake even about mathematical reasoning, I think, and much more a mistake about reason in general.

It is necessary, therefore, fundamentally to reconceive the notion of reason, whilst still thinking of reason in a way which is consistent with the objectivity of values, but which does not entail Plato's type of dogmatism and his belief that there are people who are final authorities on matters of morals and politics as well as on mathematics. How would one begin to reconstruct an account of reason to satisfy such conditions? Well, first of all, it could be argued that the values associated with reason are procedural, not substantive. In other words when one is talking about the development of reason what is important is not *just* the attaining of particular conclusions, or achieving some final state of understanding. Of course one needs to reach conclusions; for what is the point of inquiring about anything if one does not want to find out what is true? It is often said that we must not worry about giving children information; we must teach them how to acquire it for themselves. But if they do not acquire information in the end, what is the point of teaching them how to acquire it? And there must be some *value* in the acquiring of information, or it would be pointless to teach children how to acquire it. Similarly there is value in getting people to understand things. But it is not just the achievement of understanding that matters; it is also the way of going about things, which includes its own values. If the development of reason is valued, then value must be accorded to consistency, to impartiality, and to those virtues – for instance, accuracy, clarity – which are conceptually connected with the pursuit of truth. Included, also, in our wider notion of reasonableness are principles like that of freedom and respect for persons as possible sources of points of view which may be right. A certain kind of humility is also required, an acknowledgement of the possibility that anyone, above all oneself, may be in error. What matters is that one should get more and more clear about the issue rather than straining for the state of absolute certainty which was Plato's ideal.

Given that one gives a different account of reason along these lines, I think that one may have also to make the point that the principles involved in the use of reason are plural. There are the intellectual virtues that I have mentioned such as a love of consistency and clarity, impartiality, and a hatred of irrelevance and arbitrariness. There are also the other virtues which provide the social context for the exercise of reason, like respect for persons and freedom, without which this kind of social procedure could not in fact get off the ground. These groups of principles are plural in that there is not a slide-rule or Vision of Good by means of which conflicts can be reconciled. It seems to me, for instance, that freedom may conflict sometimes with impartiality. That there is some Vision of the Good, some one principle by means of which all these different principles can be unified, I think is highly questionable, though some have looked to human happiness or to justice to perform such a unifying role.

Finally, what of the supreme value of certain goods which Plato stressed? There is, for instance, his argument for the supreme value of theoretical pursuits. A case, perhaps, can be made for saying that some sort of pursuits are qualitatively superior to others – for example, that poetry is preferable to push-pin, to take the classic case. Types of activities may have features in virtue of which they are to be preferred to other types. But within these classes, for example, scientific pursuits as distinct from musical ones, or engineering as distinct from farming, it might be difficult to rank preferences. In other words there may well be a kind of pluralism again with respect to goods as well as with respect to the principles which are constitutive of the use of reason.

What then are the consequences of these criticisms? First of all the account of the development of reason must be revised. There must be much more stress on criticism and on humility, on the possibility of error, on the co-operative nature of reason, which must not be viewed just as the prerogative of the elite. Secondly, the political institutions in which reason is immanent must be fostered. Here I agree with Plato, that you cannot expect reason to develop in a social vacuum. Social life is mirrored in the individual mind and vice versa. But I would say that it is democracy, not aristocracy, which is the articulation of reason in its social form. In this revised conception of reason, democracy is the best approximation to the social form in which reason appears. For democracy at very least involves 'parlement' or discussion in the making of public decisions. And procedural principles such as freedom, impartiality and respect for persons, which structure the social context in which reason operates, are also principles immanent in the democratic way of life.

REFERENCES: CHAPTER 1

1 See Peters, R.S. 'Education and the educated man', in Peters, R.S., *Education and the Education of Teachers* (London: Routledge & Kegan Paul, 1977).

Chapter 2

The Paradoxes in Rousseau's *Emile*

INTRODUCTION

Rousseau's *Emile*, in spite of or because of its literary rather than philosophical form of presentation, has proved to be one of the most influential works in educational thought. Not only did it directly influence educationalists such as Pestalozzi and Froebel, but the writings of modern radicals such as Illich and Reimer resonate with ideas which were much more graphically presented by Rousseau. There are few who read *Emile* from cover to cover; for it is a long and discursive book. But it abounds in aphorisms and perceptive pronouncements which have been strung together in countless collections on the history of educational thought. It is the appeal of the aphorisms and the attitudes which constitutes the spell of Rousseau rather than the overall thrust of the book which is stoical rather than radical.

What then are the main themes in *Emile* which have inflamed the imaginations of so many? First of all, obviously, that he ostensibly put the child at the centre of the educational stage rather than the curriculum or the teacher. It would actually be more accurate to say that he put the boy there rather than the child; for his views about education for girls differed markedly from that outlined for Emile. Sophie is to be brought up with just the skills necessary to be a fit companion for Emile, together with the attitudes appropriate to her destiny. Rousseau was vehement with indignation at the way in which children, himself included, were then treated. They were not permitted to enjoy their childhood, but fitted into a straightjacket from the minute that they were swaddled in infancy, with what they were to become firmly in view.

The second appeal of *Emile* is that, like Rousseau's *Social Contract*, it is a sustained plea for freedom. But whereas the *Social Contract* attempts to depict an ideal society in which an individual can retain his freedom whilst fully participating in it and helping to formulate its General Will, *Emile* is an exercise in negative education, at least in its early stages. It attempts to sketch how a boy can be prepared for independence and integrity, so that he can survive in a corrupt society without becoming corrupt himself. It has echoes of the problem put to Socrates in *The Republic* about the position of the just man in the unjust society. It links with the modern aim of autonomy in education, appropriate in the 'restless and uneasy spirit of our times'; but the social context of the modern emphasis is the diversity of moral convictions above a certain level rather than widespread corruption.

The third, much more diffuse and romantic, theme in *Emile* is the glorification of Nature. Education is the development of the individual's natural tendencies; its methods must rely more on Nature than on men; Emile must be brought up in natural surroundings in the countryside; Nature provides standards of conduct, for 'the first impulses of Nature are always right'.[1] And so on. It is obvious enough, even if we confined ourselves just to the above appeals to Nature, that 'Nature' is being used in different ways. Sometimes it obviously means 'innate'. At other times it is used as a contrast to what is artificial or contrived. In other contexts it seems to single out what is spontaneous or authentic as opposed to what is premeditated or feigned. There is also the suggestion, on occasions, of less sophisticated and civilised – understandable enough in the aftermath of various explorers and their superficial reports of more 'natural' ways of living. 'Natural' is thus to be understood in Rousseau as a vague ideal to be contrasted with a number of current trends and practices which he deplored.

These, then, are the three dominant themes of *Emile*. I propose now, to take them one by one and to subject them to critical and constructive scrutiny. This will not take the form of criticising him because he was unfamiliar with Piaget's stages of development or Freud's speculations about young children. Rather it will consist mainly in assessing the internal coherence of his romance and in trying to make explicit the ambivalences from which it seems to suffer. I shall claim, for instance, that Rousseau is half-hearted in his demand that the child should be allowed to enjoy the pleasures appropriate to his age, that the role of the tutor in helping the child to attain independence turns out to be counter-productive, that there is a mystery in Rousseau's account of the natural promptings that lead him to morality as a child and the 'conscience' that is later awakened in adolescence, and that the methods of learning from Nature and things are so contrived and controlled that even Skinner might be envious.

(1) THE IDEOLOGY OF CHILDHOOD

Rousseau enunciated his foremost theme in his Preface: 'The wisest writers devote themselves to what a man ought to know, without asking what a child is capable of learning. They are always looking for the man in the child, without considering what he is before he becomes a man.'[2] The future of any child is uncertain; so why burden him with all sorts of restrictions on his present pleasures for the sake of some far-off happiness that he may never live to enjoy? 'Love childhood, indulge its sports, its pleasures, its delightful instincts.'³ A man must be treated as a man and a child as a child. Children have their own ways of seeing, thinking and feeling: it is the height of folly to try to encumber them with adult ways. 'Hold childhood in reverence and do not be in any hurry to judge it for good or ill.'⁴ Childhood is the sleep of reason; so do not worry if young children spend most of their time playing. Try to teach the child what is of use to him and that will take all your time. 'A child knows he must become a man; all the ideas he may have as to man's estate are so many opportunities for his instruction, but he should remain in complete ignorance of those ideas which are beyond his grasp. My whole book is one continued argument in support of this fundamental principle of education.'⁵ The exception to this doctrine of 'readiness' is Rousseau's nervousness about sexuality. He insists that the emergence of the sexual appetites should be delayed as long as possible to give Emile the experience to cope with them wisely. His environment is to be strictly controlled to minimise the opportunities for these powerful passions to be inflamed.

It is significant that in most of these passages Rousseau refers to 'childhood' rather than to actual children. It suggests a romantic type of ideology rather than a concern for individual children. 'Childhood' is actually ill-defined both at the beginning when Emile is taken away from his parents and entrusted to his tutor, and at the end, at the onset of adolescence, when Rousseau depicts changes occurring – for example, the development of reasoning which in fact develops continuously through 'childhood'. He singles out a mythical period when children are alleged to be creatures of sensation and practical interests and when they can be happy because their desires do not outrun their powers to satisfy them. To exist is to feel. 'Life consists less in the length of days than in the keen sense of living.'⁶ Reasoning and memory militate against this keen sense of the enjoyment of living which is typified in the play of childhood.

In actual fact, however, Rousseau's proposals for Emile's education are ambivalent. On the one hand he wants him to enjoy life as a child; but on the other hand he contrives a highly 'unnatural' life for him in the interest of developing a man that will escape corruption. His proposal, for instance, that he should be isolated from other children, to avoid the development of 'amour propre' that is born of comparison, and put in the charge of a single tutor, is not particularly consistent with his adulation of childhood; for actual children enjoy playing with other children much more than solitary play. It is true that he recommends that the tutor should be a young man, and thus more congenial as a companion to Emile than an older one, but he also says that the tutor should make himself as much like a 'thing' as possible, to make his learning more natural. This isolation, together with the various precepts suggested for the tutor, are not out of concern for the actual child, but are negative defences against Emile growing up corrupt. Or, like the proposal that Emile should learn the practical trade of carpentry, they are a mixture of proposals that suit his 'nature' and will stand him in good stead in later life. Rousseau, too, though adamantly opposed to threatening the child or giving him orders, says nothing of the child's need for affection and praise. The criticism of this omission is not that he ignores 'positive reinforcement' as an aid to learning; for whatever its efficacy, Rousseau was critical of learning to please others; it is rather that he ignores one of the most 'natural' needs of the child and thus shows lack of respect for children in their own right. There is also the point that praise and approval are most potent sources of self-respect which is an important aspect of Rousseau's ideal of the self-reliant individual. Rousseau could hardly have avoided this ambivalence if he was concerned with educating Emile; for by education we mean learning that contributes to someone becoming a person of a certain sort. So, while respecting childhood, as an educator one cannot treat children as living in the present only. The enjoyment of children must not be sacrificed in the cause of what they are to become. But their enjoyments, interests and aptitudes must be developed along desirable lines.

Rousseau's ideology of childhood is to be understood partly as a protest against the neglect of the child's point of view and the tendency to treat children just as adults in the making. More positively it is an idealisation of a more 'natural' form of life which the development of civilisation had made impossible. Children, at least in the abstract, seemed capable of enjoying this innocent carefree sort of life. I say 'in the abstract' advisedly, because Rousseau says explicitly that Emile is to be considered as 'man in the abstract'.[7] He idealised childhood but, as is clear from his account of his experiences as a tutor in his *Confessions*, actual children probably exasperated him. The fact, too, that he probably handed over the five which he fathered to a foundling hospital, does not suggest much in the way of love of children. Childhood to Rousseau was what 'the working man' has been to many intellectual socialists – an idealised object of respect, not a creature of flesh and blood to be welcomed at home.

(2) FREEDOM AND NEGATIVE EDUCATION

It is a commonplace that Rousseau's writings inspired some of the French revolutionaries who, in the cause of liberty, fraternity and equality, rebelled against the corruption and inequalities of the existing social order. But they must have taken their ideas from Rousseau's *Discourse on Inequality* and *Social Contract*, not from *Emile*; for in

Emile the ideal put forward is not revolutionary. Like A.S. Neill later, he was concerned with developing an independent and self-regulating man. Neill linked this very much, as did Rousseau, with his conception of happiness. But he stressed, more than Neill, the importance of such an individual's being able to survive in a corrupt society, an individual who can preserve his 'authentic self' by thinking for himself, and yet live on friendly terms with those who had not escaped corruption. 'Natural man' lacks the wants produced by the normal social intercourse of his day. He will have only wants that he can satisfy for himself. But there are no longer any 'natural men'. But Rousseau thought it possible, by education, to produce a man who is 'free' in the sense that he is not contaminated by social intercourse and makes only demands on others that are just. Rousseau, in *Emile*, accepts the inequalities of society. Emile will have to be born of rich parents who can afford to employ a tutor to supervise his education. But these inequalities, and the corruption which they bring in their wake, are the context which gives point to Rosseau's conception of freedom and negative education.

For Rousseau there was not necessarily any conflict between freedom and the acceptance of authority. Indeed, the benign authority of the tutor is necessary for Emile to attain freedom. This, for Rousseau, was not a matter of doing as one pleases but of not being compelled to do what one does not wish to do. Thus the tutor, who is the only model available to the child, exercises his authority by structuring Emile's learning environment, not by directly imposing his will on him. He is never authoritarian; he demonstrates and manipulates. To use Carl Rogers's recent, if not very illuminating, distinction: he does not 'teach' but is a 'facilitator' of learning.[8] He refrains from giving orders and eschews punishment, relying on the 'natural' consequences of Emile's misdemeanours. His skill lies in the control of events. He carefully chooses what is shown to Emile as soon as he is capable of taking notice – the modern doctrine of 'readiness'. In so far as Emile is 'forced to be free' it is by being put in situations where he has to learn for himself. There are, however, limits to this. Emile will not be left in high places, on his own near a fire, or within reach of dangerous weapons. And though he will be encouraged in the 'natural' practice of going about with bare feet, the tutor will make sure that there is no broken glass around![9] Rousseau even says that the tutor will 'not take pains to prevent Emile hurting himself'.[10] But it transpires that this is not in the cause of the development of independence, but because Rousseau believed that children should grow accustomed to pain.

In opposition to obedience to the tutor Rousseau does not, like many progressives, give unqualified support to following the interests and curiosity of the child, though he frequently praises these forms of motivation to learn. But he puts equal stress on the role of necessity.

The child must be brought to see the necessity for a course of action before he should be expected to embark on it. Force may have to be used to make necessity apparent on occasions. Rousseau allows the tutor at the end to tell Emile with refreshing frankness that all that 'you have gained has been won by force or guile'.[11] The tutor thus manipulates and, at times, coerces Emile until he himself develops those rational abilities which, through the foresight and example of the tutor, have been in control of him all along. So, just as in the *Social Contract*, the General Will of the community works through the individual so that he can be his 'real self', so in *Emile* the ever-present, though often concealed, authority of the tutor works through Emile in his development towards authenticity and independence. So authority of the right sort was crucial to Rousseau's conception of education. In this respect he was poles apart from some of his progressive followers. What he was opposed to was the corrupt use of authority and to devices such as giving orders and making pronouncements that were obeyed or believed because of their source rather than because of their sense.

His conviction, as expressed in *Emile*, was that this benign sort of authority, as represented by the tutor, is essential to protect the child from the corruption of society and to strengthen him so that he will emerge to independence. This consummation is slightly sullied at the end of the book; for Emile, fully grown and about to become a father, still feels the need of the tutor to take over the care of his son. Also, when his tutor resigns, he says that another will undertake his duties; for Sophie will be his guardian. (Rousseau was impressed by the immense power of women over men.) Furthermore, in an unfinished sequel to *Emile*, Emile and Sophie are unable to cope with the difficulties that befall them when the tutor departs. Emile behaves stoically, as his education has prepared him to do, but does not know what to do to save their marriage and their happiness. What the moral of this is, when compared with the confidence of *Emile*, is difficult to say.

There is the same rather negative emphasis in Rousseau's treatment of the sphere of belief of the free man as there is in the sphere of action. He is not deluded by the opinions of others. All his learning is through his own experience . Thus ignorance through lack of experience is not so culpable as error, which derives from the acceptance of the opinion of others. A potent source of inauthenticity is reliance on books and symbols which are beyond the child's experience. 'Keep the child dependent on things only.'[12] 'Let the child do nothing because he is told; nothing is good for him but what he recognises as good. When you are always urging him beyond his present understanding, you think that you are exercising a foresight which you really lack. To provide him with useless tools which he may never require, you deprive him of man's most useful tool – common sense'[13]

This free man of Rousseau's is surely both an unheroic and an improbable figure. First, he has to learn to damp down his desires to the level of his powers to satisfy them; he also has to be submissive, not just to necessity but also to his tutor, who may on occasions have to make necessity apparent to him. This submissiveness he carries over into later life. He is to be a man of integrity but not a rebel. Secondly, he has to enter a world structured with the opinions and demands of others, but has no experience of coping with them; for his tutor arranges for him to find out everything for himself. He never presents opinions, whether true or false, which Emile is encouraged to criticise and discuss. The antidote to credulity, which Rousseau regarded as one of the greatest enemies, is not just first-hand experience. It is also the development of the criticial spirit and training in argument and discussion. But there are no such training situations in *Emile*; for the tutor knows all the answers and just uses various devices to get Emile to see them. Rousseau thought error worse than ignorance. But errors serve a very important function, as J.S. Mill was later to argue, in that public discussion of them promotes a closer approximation to what is true. Finally Emile will emerge from his education with a somewhat warped and idealistic view of the role of authority. He will recognise the difference between acting in accordance with the dictates of someone in authority and doing things because they are laid down by authority. For he will see the sense of what his wise tutor requests. But he will only experience situations in which the necessity of what is requested is apparent. But in society those in authority lay down all sorts of things the rationale for which is often difficult for the ordinary man to discern. If the authority structure is a rational one and those in authority have been given the right, through legitimate procedures, to legislate or give orders, the citizen is under a *prima facie* obligation to obey, even if he is unclear about the necessity. Footballers, if they are wise, do not ponder about necessity when the captain gives an order in the middle of a game. Thus Emile would only be at home in a society like that sketched in the *Social Contract* where, in theory at any rate, the citizens, by participation, grasp the rationale of the laws. He would not be at all at home in the corrupt hierarchy in which he had to maintain his integrity.

(3) THE IDEALISATION OF NATURE

The common theme running through all Rousseau's various appeals to Nature is enunciated at the start of *Emile*: 'God made all things good; man meddles with them and they become evil . . . he will have nothing as nature made it, not even man himself, who must learn his paces like a saddle-horse, and be shaped in his master's taste like the trees in his garden.'[14] Man has certain natural, or innate, tendencies, and everything should be brought into harmony with them. Education is not concerned with training for any particular profession, 'Life is the trade I would teach him.'[15] We begin to learn when we begin to live. This is cramped from the start by the iniquitous practice of swaddling. Nature has her own way of hardening children by pain, grief and disease. Indeed, only half of them survive. Doctors do more harm than good and infect us with credulity, timidity and the fear of death. Emile will not have one unless his life is in danger, when the doctor can only kill him. Manual labour and life in the natural surroundings of the countryside are a much better defence against disease.

Rousseau held an ill-defined theory of the development of the child's nature. The years between 2 and 12 are of central importance when the senses develop and the mind should be left undisturbed. In these years the emphasis should be on preserving the heart from vice and the spirit from error. The body should be exercised and the senses sharpened but the mind should be kept idle. 'Leave childhood to ripen in your children.'[16] At pre-adolescence (12–15) practical problem-solving is stressed; geography and elementary science related to Emile's practical interests and needs are to be encouraged. He is to learn a trade, carpentry, and is to be allowed to read *Robinson Crusoe*. His reason is developing and he must be given opportunities for making elementary inferences. At adolescence his sexual impulses can no longer be contained (16–20). They open the way to more refined moral feelings, especially compassion. His conscience matures and he enters society fortified by natural religion, aesthetic subjects and a study of history. At 20 he is introduced to Sophie who is to be his wife and 'guardian' and to take over from his tutor. At this point the book becomes rather like a romantic novel but returns at the end to the finishing of Emile's education with tutorials in political theory, travel, studying different governments, and so on, until he returns to marry Sophie and to retire to a farm in the country. In spite of this somewhat bizarre method of acquiring his intellectual equipment, in content it does not differ markedly from that of the eighteenth-century ideal of the liberally educated man.

Rousseau's view that 'childhood is the sleep of reason' and that nothing should be done about developing it until pre-adolescence sounds a bit quaint. But he seems to have meant abstract reasoning – what Piaget called 'formal operations'. Obviously children would have to employ more concrete forms of reason in planning means to ends and making practical inferences. This doctrine derived from Locke's sensationism, according to which sensations give rise to images and abstract ideas are developed by the mind operating on the images. Relationships are discerned between the abstract ideas which are the starting points for reasoning. It is not, therefore. worth trying to fathom quite what Rosseau's version was of this long-discarded theory. Of more interest is what he said about learning from and through experience.

Children, thought Rousseau, are naturally curious, which is to be distinguished sharply from the desire to be learned. So whatever knowledge has no natural attraction for the child should be omitted from his studies. Instinct is to be his guide. 'No book but the word, no teaching but that of fact. The child who reads ceases to think, he only reads. He is acquiring words, not knowledge. Let him not be taught science, let him discover it. If ever you substitute authority for reason he will cease to reason; he will be a mere plaything of other people's thoughts.'[17] Symbols unrelated to the child's experience are as great an enemy to his authenticity as the dictates of authority. The ruin of children begins with the first thing taken for granted on the word of another without the child's seeing its use for himself. Nature, not man, is to be his schoolmaster and he learns quicker because he does not know that he has a lesson to learn. The child will thus think that his progress is due to his own efforts; and indeed it will be. But the tutor will have carefully arranged the natural situations to which Emile is exposed. Indeed he should not take one step that the tutor has not foreseen, nor utter a word that the tutor could not foretell.

The tutor will not teach Emile geometry; Emile will teach himself by drawing accurate figures, superimposing them, and discovering their relations. The whole of elementary geometry will be revealed by passing from one observation to another without a word of definitions or problems. But this will not happen by chance; it will be the product of clever contrivance by the tutor. In a similar way Emile will be guided to discover that sound travels more slowly than the sight of an explosion, the properties of magnetism, the workings of the compass and the thermometer. So all the laws of statics and hydrostatics will be discovered by rough experiments. 'The scientific atmosphere destroys science.'[18] Verbal explanations are a hindrance. 'Things! Things! I cannot repeat it too often. We lay too much stress on words; we teachers babble, and our scholars follow our example.'[19] Gradually, if these methods are followed, Emile will develop ideas out of sensations, and will be able to reason as well as to feel. He will not be learned; but he will know how to learn.

This indictment could be continued indefinitely, but it would be just a series of variations on the same themes. Its significance and its perennial importance lie more in its polemical attacks than in its positive proposals. Indeed most progressive writings have to be understood – and commended – largely in terms of what they are said against. Their positive panaceas may have some merits but are usually not generalisable because they relate to small schools with special children and a very favourable teacher–pupil ratio, like those of Dewey, Susan Isaacs, Neill and Pestalozzi. Rousseau outdid them all by suggesting one tutor for each child. But then Emile was just 'man in the abstract'.

But what of the intrinsic merits and demerits of his proposals, granted that his protests against empty formalism, rote learning, premature instruction, lack of relevance of learning to life, and so on, were amply justified and are to be applauded without qualification. There is, of course, the first and obvious criticism that what is natural is not necessarily good, whichever of the many meanings is attached to 'natural'. To commend something simply because it is natural presupposes the general assumption either that 'natural' means good or desirable or that being natural is an indisputable ground of desirability. And obviously it is not. Suppose aggression is natural in the sense of innate. Its innateness would not confer desirability upon it any more than it would confer it on sympathy. However, it is otiose to dwell at greater length on Rousseau's grand-scale commission of the naturalistic fallacy.

Of more interest is the fact that Rousseau, in the educational field, wants Nature and things to do the work; but they do not do the work on their own. Emile does not roam aimlessly around learning as he goes; the things and aspects of Nature are carefully arranged for him by the tutor. It is true that Rousseau says that the tutor, too, must become like a 'thing' in so far as he does not instruct and tell Emile things. But he foresees every step Emile takes and foretells all that he will utter. In other words Nature is only indirectly doing the teaching. The real teacher is the tutor and he is using Nature as a modern teacher might use sand and water to aid the child's understanding. The difference is that the situation is envisaged as being much more supervised and controlled than that of any child in a modern progressive school. This extremely directive role of the tutor is seldom stressed by those who quote Rousseau with the most enthusiasm. Nature and things are tamed to act as teachers! Far be it from me to comment on the merits or demerits of this highly structured type of learning. I am only commenting on Rousseau's ambivalence on the importance of 'men' as distinct from 'Nature' and 'things' as the main source of Emile's education.

Once Emile has been put in the way of learning by being confronted with an appropriate thing or aspect of nature, Rousseau's story of what is likely to happen suffers from two defects which he inherited from Locke's sensationism. He assumes that nature will as it were register itself on Emile's senses uncorrupted by the conventions of society. But this is an absurdity. As Kant put it 'percepts without concepts are blind' or, to use the more modern idiom, 'all seeing is seeing as'. He had been brought up in a family and would have learnt, even before he learnt to talk, to impose a certain type of conceptual framework on his experience. Also he would not approach nature like a piece of blotting paper waiting to soak up what he saw. He would have implicit or explicit expectations which would be confirmed or falsified. Rousseau made the usual empiricist mistake of confusing the valid point that assumptions about the world, however arrived at, must be tested by sensory observation, with the invalid point that they must originate from sense observation. And he did not appreciate that this appeal to experience is not itself a 'natural' tendency; it is the product of a social tradition. In the history of man the more 'natural' (universal) tendency is to rely on hearsay and tradition. Man has an inveterate tendency to predict events, to generalise on the basis of slender experience. Events may prove him false. But science proper does not develop until man systematically sets about falsifying his predictions. This determination to counteract what William James called the 'primacy of belief' is the product of a social tradition. It is not just a matter of natural accommodation. Miseducation springs as much from taking Nature at its face value as it does from believing what we are told.

To a certain extent the tutor, by arranging the environment so that Emile will make mistakes, encourages in Emile a trial-and-error attitude. But he does not encourage the determined search for the negative instance, on which Bacon and later Popper put so much emphasis in their accounts of scientific method. Emile is usually led ingeniously by the tutor to make discoveries – for example, of magnetism with the elaborate experiment with the duck. But though he is protected from the credulity which comes from accepting other people's opinions, he has no training in scepticism, in systematically checking his own 'discoveries' under varying conditions. There is also no attempt to move beyond the simple generalisations implicit in the discoveries of magnetism, the thermometer, and so on, to theories which might explain them. No doubt Rousseau, if he knew the theories, was concerned only with discoveries which might be deemed of practical use.

Rousseau insists throughout that learning must arise from Emile's interests, instincts, needs, and so on. He must never be forced to do what he does not want to do. He is particularly averse to emulating others and dismisses imitation as unworthy. But how many interests are 'natural' in the sense of innate? Most interests, surely, arise from peers, parents and teachers. And it is highly improbable that Emile, with his tutor as his sole companion for so many years – and a companion whom, by definition, he loves and admires – would not imitate him, even though he tries to make himself like a 'thing', and, by identification, acquire most of his interests from him. There is nothing reprehensible in that, except in terms of Rousseau's theory. However implausible Rousseau's doctrine of natural interests and of learning at first hand from nature may seem to us, he is surely to be credited with considerable insight, which is a commonplace today amongst sociologists of knowledge, namely, the enormous influence of other people, whom he regarded as corrupted, on people's views of the world and their interests and attitudes. He suggested heroic, if impracticable, measures to counteract these influences, so that Emile would be untainted by what Dewey called the 'social milieu'. But he is at least to be given credit for seeing the extent to which the individual mind is the product of the prevailing social consciousness.

Rousseau, however, was not a sentimentalist about children's interests like many later progressives. The tutor may deliberately let Emile pursue interests that lead into blind alleys, so that he may really learn a lesson instead of just being discouraged by his tutor. Or he may put him in the way of situations where his interests have the sorts of features which Dewey later ascribed to educative experiences; they have continuity, there is mileage in them. The situation of Emile, of course, evades the basic problem of this precept for learning, which is that of the pupil–teacher ratio which, in mass education, makes such individualised learning so difficult to contrive. It also avoids the variations in the social consciousness of the homes from which children come; for so many disadvantaged children come to school with few interests on which the teacher can build.

Rousseau's emphasis on interest and learning from Nature is the obverse side of his distrust of instruction and books. His denunciation of books is difficult to understand; for he himself was more or less self-educated by means of them. He objected to both, partly because they encouraged vanity, illusion and credulity, and partly because they were vehicles for useless knowledge – both of which could be avoided if the study of nature was prompted by natural interest. These objections are surely largely contingent on Rousseau's assessment of current practices. Instruction can take the form of explanation and questioning; it need not take the form of rote learning, sermonising and dictation. And, in the hands of an articulate and enthusiastic teacher, children's curiosity may be aroused and new interests stimulated. Also it is difficult to see how skills, such as carpentry, can be learnt without instruction and example. Books, too, may be a source of fascination rather than of toil to appear learned. They may stimulate the imagination and take the individual beyond the confines of the here and now where Rousseau wanted children to linger because of their unrepeatable enjoyment of it. Progressives have a horror of children being told anything. But, assuming they want to know what they are told, and assuming, too, that they are encouraged to be critical of what they hear, there seems no more indignity in telling them directly than in elaborately contriving a situation so that they will find out for themslves. This often means, in practice, that they have to go and consult a book anyway, as only a limited number of children's questions can be answered by adopting Rousseau's methods. It is said that they will learn how to learn by these methods. There are two points to be made about this cliché that is as popular now as it was with Rousseau. First, there is no point in learning how to learn unless something is eventually learnt. Secondly, a critical scrutiny of what other people say as well as what is recorded in books plays as important a part in learning how to learn as contriving natural experiments. Rousseau also ignores the most important form of knowledge for most human beings – that of other people and their motives and aspirations. Such knowledge cannot be obtained by 'natural' methods.

The 'practical use' emphasis in Rousseau is ambiguous. Did he mean what the child sees as practically useful or what the tutor, with foresight of the future, sees as practically useful? If the former, then the child may never see the practical use of something like reading without the mastery of which he will be severely handicapped. If the latter, the question has to be asked 'useful for what?'. Obviously, for instance, Emile's mastery of carpentry will be useful in his earning a living. But for what is that useful? To keep Sophie and their child? For what? So that their child may become a carpenter too? The point of constructing this roundabout is to bring out that there must be some stopping point to the instrumental question. Without this being specified the appeal to 'practical use' is nebulous. The ideal of personal or social good that constitutes such a stopping point may well itself contain the practice of what is being learnt. One of the best reasons for learning philosophy is so that one can think philosophically about one's life. Indeed, unless some things that are learnt fall into this category, work and learning are going to be alienated, pursuits with which the individual cannot identify himself.

Rousseau did not discuss such ultimate issues. He was carried away by indignation at the remoteness from life of most instruction and book learning. He was intent that Emile 'learn the trade of life'. So only practical geography is permitted in pre-adolescence and some history later on to help him understand the governments of countries that he visits. But what sort of life is a human being to lead with such a myopic vision of his place in the world, so limited a knowledge of its great variety of men and their diverse habitations, and so mundane an awareness of his place in the historical order? Education requires distancing man from the immediate here and now as well as relating him to it. It must provide a conceptual framework within which the 'practically useful' can be located. It must arouse wonder and awe as well as curiosity and interest. For all its romantic qualities, *Emile* is deficient on the development of the imagination. Emile was to be forbidden access to imaginative literature. Rousseau associated this with fantasies and illusions which would foster role-playing and *amour propre* in Emile instead of insightful self-love and authenticity.

(4) MORAL EDUCATION

There is finally the puzzle about Rousseau's account of the 'natural' development of morality. He believed that self-love was the basic 'natural' tendency underlying man's conduct, including his morality. This could be extended to pity for those in unfortunate circumstances which he himself had experienced. His unreasonable wishes must be met with physical obstacles only, or the 'punishment' which results from his own actions. The place of law should be taken by experience or lack of power. Emile is basically self-centred, but he will come across others like Robert the gardener who also have wants and who are more powerful than he. He will see the necessity of taking account of such facts of his situation – especially as he will live mainly among adults. He will realise that he cannot rely on others to get what he wants and so will either have to rely on himself or win their goodwill to help him. So the direction taken by self-love will depend upon circumstances. If due account is taken of the wants of others, gradually a code approximating to 'do as you would be done by' will emerge. If, however, he is ordered around and bullied, he will resort to deceit and malice to assert himself. If he is brought up with other children comparison with them may lead to competition, vanity and all the evils which Rousseau associated with *amour propre*. In his view *amour propre* which develops though being susceptible to the opinions which others hold of us is the source of most of the base passions that afflict us. If, on the other hand, the child who is born innocent rather than good or bad (which are absurdities) is brought up as Rousseau suggests, though he may behave in an anti-social way at times, he will not do so with evil intent. Hopefully pity will be developed which is the natural tendency that binds him to others. This will be extended by reflection and imagination. Eventually, he suggests, when Emile enters society, an appropriate form of *amour propre* may be imposed on his *amour de soi-même*, which is not the product of chance social influences but of the extension, through reason, of his original self-love. This will come about largely through his realisation of his own insufficiency and his pity for others in the same plight.

Rousseau's thesis that self-love will take a desirable course because 'natural consequences' which Emile will accept, rather than human disapproval, which he will resent, will act as correctives, is both disingenuous and impractical. It is disingenuous because the tutor carefully arranges most of the 'natural consequences'; so they are not properly 'natural'. It is impractical because the *natural* consequences of misdemeanours such as cruelty, cheating and lying do not seem obvious. And Rousseau wished to avoid the probable social consequences such as disapproval which they would occasion. Rousseau only makes his doctrine look plausible by taking examples like breaking windows. He makes sure that Emile is not put in a position where he could commit arson or shoot anyone! Emile's isolation from his peers removes him from the context in which the beginnings of morality develop. He does say elsewhere that children learn more from each other than from adults, but nothing is made of this insight in *Emile*. His environment is a mixture of Nature and a few adults.

This account of moral development is highly implausible but has a certain consistency about it. However, in Book IV a Savoyard priest is introduced to reveal to Emile the ultimate mysteries of morality and natural religion which he will need to grasp before being ready to enter society. One of his central convictions is that man is 'naturally' endowed with a conscience which emerges gradually as man comes to maturity. It is not the product of upbringing, for it 'persists in following the order of nature, in spite of all the laws of man'.[20] It is an 'innate principle of justice and virtue';[21] so it cannot be the product of Rousseau's system of training self-love by natural consequences. Indeed, what is the function of this elaborate early training if conscience is going to emerge anyway as the end-point of a process of natural maturation, rather like the sex organs at puberty?

There is little point in raising all the difficulties that moral philosophers have explored both about the existence of such an inner faculty and about the identifiability and reliability of its pronouncements. My concern is only with Rousseau's account of natural education. My point is that in the moral sphere a highly implausible account of moral education is rendered otiose by the appearance, at the end, of an innate sense of right and wrong, like a *deus ex machina* to link natural man with the order laid down by his creator. The explanation may well be that *Emile* reads more like a collection of themes than a unified book. There is the courtship of Sophie by Emile, the discourse of the Savoyard priest, the eulogy of childhood, the part on natural education, the finishing of Emile's education at the end. It may well be that, if the book was put together in this rather disjointed way, Rousseau failed to discern the inconsistency between the Savoyard priest piece, whose views on religion led to his having to flee from the country, and the earlier part on natural education in which moral education was included. But as it stands it seems difficult to reconcile the emergence of an innate conscience with the elaborate training necessary for Emile's sense of self-preservation to develop into the type of self-reliance that makes only just demands on others and withstands corruption.

CONCLUSION

It is time to draw to a close by attempting to estimate the lasting contribution of Rousseau to educational theory. He was not the first (cf. Plato) to advocate relating learning to the conceptual development and interests of the child; but his sustained eulogy of childhood and his somewhat forced separation of it from adolescence brought this home vividly to later generations of educators. Rousseau, as it were, put childhood on the map as a generally accepted entity. Nowadays it would probably be called a 'social construct'!

Secondly, though his appeal to nature, natural development and natural methods was rather like More's *Utopia* – an idealisation of the opposite of current practices to which he objected in a corrupt society – his eloquence in denouncing formalism, book-learning beyond the experience of children and repressive methods of moral training was salutary enough. Though Nature may be as unreliable a guide as men, and just as likely to engender credulity, it is not as likely to dampen interest and curiosity as interminable instruction. Rousseau's stress, at the pre-adolescent period, on the practical use of what can be learnt from books is, as has been shown, ambiguous. There are echoes of it in Dewey's attempt to marry the 'impulses' of the child with his cultural inheritance. But if 'use' is interpreted in relation to his declaration that 'life is the trade I would teach him', this is surely what education is concerned with – not 'inert ideas', but knowledge, understanding, attitudes and sensitivities that have relevance to the human condition. Rousseau saw, too, that education, so understood, was not incompatible with learning a trade. This conviction is very relevant to modern controversies.

Thirdly, Rousseau combined an emphasis on the experience and interests of the child with an understanding of the importance of authority. Although opposed to authoritarianism and the imposition of orders on the child, he appreciated that a learning situation must involve authority of some sort. The question is whether it is to be manipulative and implicit rather than coercive and explicit. Rousseau advocated the former. The role of the tutor is to arrange learning experiences for the child and to get him to do only those things that he sees reasons for doing. But at times, in his anxiety that Emile will avoid corruption, Rousseau seems to lack any trust in him. He should never take a step that the tutor had not foreseen, nor utter a word that he could not foretell. And at the end, when the tutor tells Emile that all he has gained has been won by force and guile, the frankly manipulative character of his role is made explicit. Rousseau was franker and more perceptive than most progressives! But the fact that Emile cannot bear to be deprived of his tutor when he is married and about to have a child suggests that the surveillance has been too close.

This somewhat surprising conclusion to a non-authoritarian education is consistent with Rousseau's conception of freedom in the *Social Contract*. In both cases the individual's freedom does not consist in doing what he is superficially inclined to do but in doing what impartial reflection tells him that there are reasons for doing. He may have to be 'forced to be free' because he may be unappreciative of the necessity for a course of action. And just as in the one case there is the General

Will interpreted by the mysterious law-giver, so in the other there is the tutor to bring him to see what necessity demands. This falling short of genuine autonomy is probably a projection of Rousseau's perennial personal problem. He was a man of extreme sensitivity and vacillating inclinations whose feelings were more highly developed than his judgement. With a background of the iron laws of Geneva speaking through his guardians, when he went to Paris, with all its corruption, he felt the need for an authority more benign than that of Geneva to help him both to decide on and to persist in courses of action that were sensible and just. The negative education of Emile is an attempt to sketch how a man might be educated so as to resist corruption as he could no longer be a 'natural' man. But Rousseau's fascination for authority was such that, even in the end, he could not bring Emile to say that the tutor had finished his task. This is one of the greatest paradoxes in the most influential of all works in the progressive tradition.

REFERENCES: CHAPTER 2

1 Rousseau, J.-J., *Emile* (London: Everyman edn, Dent, 1911), p. 86.
2 ibid., p.1.
3 ibid., p. 43.
4 ibid., p. 71.
5 ibid., p. 141.
6 ibid., p. 10.
7 loc. cit.
8 Rogers, C., *Freedom to Learn* (Columbus, Ohio: Charles Merrill, 1969).
9 Rousseau, op. cit., p. 104
10 ibid., p. 41
11 ibid., p. 281
12 ibid., p. 49
13 ibid., p.141.
14 ibid., p.5.
15 ibid., p. 9.
16 ibid., p. 53.
17 ibid., p. 131.
18 ibid., p. 139.
19 ibid., p. 143.
20 ibid., p. 229.
21 ibid., p. 252.

The following articles were found helpful in constructing this one:
Plamanatz, J., 'Rousseau: the education of Emile', *Proceedings of the Philosophy of Education Society of Great Britain*, July 1972.
Shklar, Judith N., 'Rousseau's images of authority' in Cranston, M. and Peters, R.S. (eds), *Hobbes and Rousseau* (New York: Doubleday/Anchor, 1972).
Barrow, R., *Radical Education* (London; Martin Robertson, 1978), chs 2, 3.

Chapter 3

Democratic Values and Educational Aims

(1) EDUCATION

It is often said that 'education' is an essentially contested concept.[1] Like 'morality' and 'democracy', it marks out features of life that are deemed desirable, but there is no one standard usage that can be taken as a model of correctness. So different groups compete endlessly for their particular interpretations. If they attempt any kind of definition they must necessarily produce what Stevenson nearly forty years ago called a 'persuasive definition'.[2] Selected conditions are linked with a recommending type of word and by this indirect method certain policies or ways of life are given the stamp of approval.

There is much to be said for this contention; for the term *education* is used valuatively, but vaguely with lack of precision regarding its area of application. From this it might be mistakenly suggested that all that needs to be done is to pick out certain criteria that seem central to one's understanding of education and lay these down as a stipulatory preliminary to the issues to be discussed. This, I think, would be a pretty pointless and presumptuous procedure. To start with, the concept of education may be contestable, but it is not completely so. We cannot call anything we like education – for example, scratching our heads. At least it denotes some kind of *learning* – and not any kind of learning either. At one time education was more or less synonymous with the learning involved in upbringing and, according to the *Oxford English Dictionary*, was used of animals – even silkworms. As with many concepts, however, changes have taken place that mirror changes in economic and social life. Although, on occasion, the term *education* may be used to speak of the upbringing or schooling of children in a noncommittal way, it is also used with more specific suggestions. We can now say that a person has been to school but is not educated or that his upbringing was not particularly educative. Dogs bring up but do not educate their young.

What more can be said that is not contestable about these extra suggestions intimated by this conceptual shift? For the interesting point about contestable concepts, so it seems to me, is the point at which they become so. The clue to the conceptual shift in question is surely the development of industrialism in the nineteenth century. It came to be realised that it would be a benefit if the average man could read, write and perform elementary calculations. Many skills and roles, too, required a modicum of specialised knowledge if they were to be performed efficiently. What is now called 'training' became widespread, often backed up by religious instruction to 'gentle the masses'. By training is meant knowledge and skill devised to bring about some specific end; it began to be contrasted with education, which was used to speak of the beliefs, attitudes and outlook of a person *qua* person and not just in his capacity as a skilled man or the occupant of a specific role. Education thus became associated with developing the 'whole man' mainly by various forms of cognitive growth. Upbringing has neither of these suggestions. It is compatible with training a person to occupy a role, and with a narrow outlook as well.

This connection between education and the many-sided development of a person *qua* person has occasioned, in my view, two characteristic mistakes. On the one hand there are theorists like Langford[3] who equate education just with becoming a person. But education surely cannot mean as little as this; for in a straightforward sense many persons are uneducated, and, if this type of linguistic argument is thought objectionable, surely those who go to secondary schools and universities to continue their education are persons already, unless all sorts of valuative criteria are built into the concept of a 'person'. On the other hand there is Carl Bereiter[4] who, building his case on the distinction between training and education, holds that the schools have no right to educate; for this involves the moulding of the whole personality of the individual. But education surely cannot mean as much as this; for a major feature of a person's personality is his temperament, which is singularly resistant to learning. In so far, then, as education centrally implies learning, it cannot transform a person's *whole* personality.

What then can it develop over and above those minimum features necessary to become a person, but falling short of the transformation of the whole personality? Education surely develops a person's *awareness* by enlarging, deepening and extending it. Its impact is cognitive, but it also transforms and regulates a person's attitudes, emotions, wants and actions because all of these presuppose awareness and are impregnated with beliefs. Also, in so far as these are altered by learning, this comes about through the person's attending to, noticing, or understanding some feature of a situation that he copies or makes his own. And these are all forms of cognition. Of course attitudes, emotions and wants can be altered and induced by drugs, by physiological changes and by interferences with the brain. But these changes are not the product of learning; for learning implies mastering something or coming up to some standard as the result of *experience*. And the cognitive aspect of experience is fundamental in learning.

The connection with 'wholeness' stressed by Bereiter is explained by the fact that being educated is incompatible with the narrow outlook associated with being just trained for a particular job or in a particular form of awareness, though, of course, training in a skill or for a role may well form part of – even the pivotal point of – a person's education. I have sympathy, therefore, for the view expressed by a speaker at a recent conference, at which the claims of vocational training were being pressed, that the purpose of education is not to prepare people for jobs but to prepare them for life. This, however, is misleading if taken literally, for (1) presumably he meant something like a worthwhile life, not just keeping alive; (2) as Dewey so forcefully argued, education is not just a preparation for living but is continuous with it, in that we should always be prepared to learn – as William Morris put it 'learn to live, live to learn'; (3) 'life' needs further specification when contrasted with jobs. It is helpful in that it stresses that education should not consist of the accumulation of 'inert ideas' that have no application to people's lives, but it does not in any way specify the areas of application. Towards what situations, then, is the development of awareness to be directed if a person's role or occupation is not to be emphasised? The answer can only be 'the human condition'. By that I mean, first, those features of the natural world that impinge on man and those that he shares with the natural world as part of the kingdom of nature. In the former category would be included phenomena such as the seasons, storms, tides, electricity, frost, fire, and so forth; in the latter, birth, death, procreation, ageing and disease. Then, secondly, there is the interpersonal world of human affection and hate, of dominance and dependence, of friendship and loneliness. Finally, there is the economic, social and political world of poverty and affluence, authority and violence, crime and punishment, consensus and dissent. Whatever a man's occupation, it is predictable that he will be confronted with phenomena such as these. In so far, therefore, as education is concerned with learning how to live, his beliefs, attitudes, desires and emotional reactions to these spheres will have to be developed and disciplined in various ways.

But in what ways? In trying to answer this question we have surely arrived at the contestable aspect of this more specific concept of education. For filling in the respects in which a person's awareness should be enlarged, deepened, sensitised, disciplined, and so forth, depends first on the values with which a society confronts these various aspects of the human condition and secondly on the emphases selected by its educators. These emphases, as Dewey maintained, constitute aims of education, which can become part of a person's or group's concept of education, in that education means processes of learning directed towards states of mind that are thought valuable, and these specific valuations can be built into the concept. Downie and Telfer, for instance, maintain that knowledge of various kinds is the distinguishing feature of an educated person.[5] I myself, in previous writings, assigned a similar role to all-round knowledge and understanding. But this is manifestly contestable, even within our own society. For though this is *an* aim of education, it is surely a narrow one. Many people, for instance, think that forms of awareness such as the aesthetic and the religious ought to be developed; but to talk of 'knowledge' in these spheres is scarcely appropriate. Also in moral education, for example, what people do, their attitudes, actions and habits, are as important as what they know and believe. Then there is the whole area of emotional development, with which education is surely concerned. Of course beliefs, and sometimes knowledge, are constituents of actions, attitudes and emotions. But they are not the only constituents; so to confine education to the development of knowledge is to impose an unwarrantable restriction on it.

(2) AIMS OF EDUCATION

It was suggested that aims of education can be regarded as aspects of the values of a society that an educator considers necessary to emphasise at a given time. This suggests three formal points about aims. First, they must point to features of development that are thought to be desirable. Secondly, they must pick out reasonably specific goals, like targets. They lack the generality of ideals. They are also – and this is the third formal point – unlike ideals in that, whereas ideals suggest unattainability, for example, truth, universal happiness, the classless society, aims point to goals that are attainable, but with difficulty. If they are aims of education they must therefore be more or less attainable by some processes of learning, though with difficulty, for example, personal autonomy, concern for others, and so forth.

   This third point is rather an important one in that it imposes limits on what can feature as aims of education. Happiness, for instance, is almost universally yearned for as a state of mind in which one can accommodate oneself to the human condition. But could it realistically be aimed at by educators? There are three problems about this. First, education is not a necessary path to happiness, for many uneducated people are perfectly happy. Secondly, happiness is a complex state of mind depending at least upon having desires that are fulfilled and the planning and scheduling of their satisfaction so that they do not conflict, lacking fears for the future and regret or remorse about the past, and having general expectations of life that are matched by circumstances. The subjective side of happiness might be improved by education, but this is very difficult to do for someone else in a teaching-learning situation, unless one knows the other person very well, because desires and expectations can be highly idiosyncratic. But thirdly, and more important, happiness depends also on objective conditions having to do with circumstances, which may change because of events for which the individual may not be responsible, and there is nothing much that education can do about these.

It might be said that a man who is made redundant through no fault of his own, loses his wife, or has a heart attack should be able to cope better with such adversity if he is educated than if he is not. This may be so, but it is a speculative suggestion. For how a man copes with such adversity is a very individual matter depending as much on his temperament as on the quality of his awareness. Also, an educated person is likely to have higher expectations of life and of himself; so the discrepancy between his expectations and his changed circumstances is likely to be greater. And in so far as he does cope, the most he is likely to do is to minimise the misery rather than to restore his happiness. And this would be my general conclusion about the relationship of education to happiness. Education, by developing a person's awareness in various ways, may rid him of forms of ignorance, irrationality and insensitivity that stand in the way of his being happy. But because of its highly idiosyncratic character and because of the large element of luck lurking in its objective conditions, education cannot predictably promote, let alone guarantee, happiness.

If we turn from such formal points about aims to questions of their substance, we have first, so I have argued, to make explicit the values of the society in which education is taking place, and then state specific aspects of these values that we think need emphasis. Alternatively we could disapprove of certain of these values and state as aims of education what we think needs emphasis as correctives to what is commonly accepted. In either case the articulation of such values must be a preliminary to the formulation of aims. Ideally, in order to avoid the charge or arbitrariness, justifications should be offered for the values as well. But in an essay of this length I fear that that will not be possible. So I must approach aims of education by briefly sketching the basic values distinctive to the type of democratic society in which we live.

(3) DEMOCRATIC VALUES

Democracy is itself a contestable concept and I do not propose here to discuss possible interpretations of it – for example, Dewey's conception of a way of life that maximises shared experiences and openness of communication between groups. Rather I shall adopt the interpretation of it, which seems to fit this country, that I previously elaborated in *Ethics and Education*.[6] In this central importance was given to a way of life in which matters of policy are resolved, wherever possible, by discussion, *parliament* deriving from the French word for discussion.

To decide things by discussion requires truth-telling, respect for persons and the impartial consideration of interests as underlying moral principles. But it also requires the institutional underpinning of a system of representation, public accountability and freedom of speech and assembly. If these are to be more than a formal façade that can be manipulated by interest groups, something approaching Dewey's passion for 'shared experiences', together with concern for the common good, is also required to encourage widespread participation in public life. This suggests a revival of the almost forgotten ideal of fraternity to vitalise public projects as well as the ability to discuss and criticise public policy. Such criticism should be well informed and a rational attitude is required toward authority and its exercise.

Democracy, in brief, is a way of life in which high value is placed on the development of reason and principles such as freedom, truth-telling, impartiality and respect for persons, which the use of reason in social life presupposes. This development of reason would be unintelligible if value were not also accorded to the overarching ideal of truth.

In spite, however, of this firm commitment to specific values in a democracy, it will be noted that they are predominantly of a procedural sort. By that I mean that they make demands on how social, political and personal life ought to be conducted. They do not provide a blueprint for an ideal society or indicate what sort of life is most worth living. Indeed, there is a sense in which democracy manifests a certain scepticism about values in that no single conception of the good for man is acknowledged, and fallibility rather than certainty tends to be emphasised in the realm of truth. No Platonic seers are acknowledged as final authorities on such matters; they are left to public debate and individual decision. But this kind of pluralism in certain realms of value is possible only because other values such as toleration, respect for persons and impartiality are accepted as constitutive of the form of life in which it can flourish.

If we look at the set of values linked together in this conception of the democratic way of life we can, for purposes of exposition, distinguish three groups. First, there are those such as concern for others, impartiality and respect for persons that underpin procedural consensus. Secondly, there are values connected with truth, which provide point for discussion and the attempt to decide matters by reason. Thirdly – and this is really a requirement of respect for persons – there are the values associated with the pursuit of personal good. The democrat may have definite views about what constitutes this good but respect for persons requires that he should not impose it on others, nor despise others if their choice of a way of life seems bizarre. Before articulating aims of education arising from these values, however, it will be necessary to flesh them out in a little more detail.

(a) Interpersonal morality

Although a person who accepts the procedural principles of impartiality, concern for others and respect for persons will refrain from imposing some conception of personal good on others, there are two spheres in which his principles do not require such a *laissez-faire* attitude. The first is that of the necessity for a basic body of lower-order rules – for example, of non-injury, keeping contracts, respect for property whether private or public – without which a democratic society could not continue. Such basic duties can be justified by reference to the procedural principles and must be insisted on as moral duties; for the police cannot be omnipresent to enforce them as laws.

Secondly, underlying the search for personal good and the restrictions placed on it by considerations of its effect on others, there is a minimum conception of welfare demarcating the common good. By that I mean that, whatever a person's conception of good, there are certain basic conditions of welfare, the absence of which will militate against his attaining it. These would include health, both physical and mental, housing, adequate income, heat and light, transport, and so forth. But over and above this comparatively non-controversial level of minimum conditions of welfare, can anything further be said about the individual's good? For in dealing with others as well as in considering our own lives we operate with more positive conceptions.

(b) Personal good

Happiness might be regarded by many as the obvious positive constituent of personal good. But it has already been ruled out as being suitable to generate aims of education, mainly because of its connections with circumstances over which neither the individual nor the educator has much control. The next obvious suggestion, therefore, would be to cut loose the connection with circumstances and settle for individual satisfaction and self-fulfilment. But straightaway there emerges Bentham's problem of comparing the joys of poetry with those of push-pin, which was personalised by J.S. Mill in his defence of the 'quality' of pleasure of the perplexed Socrates against that of the satisfied fool. Mill, I think, was right in appealing implicitly to some standard other than a purely hedonistic one in his emphasis on quality. For it is difficult to construct a convincing defence for Socrates purely in hedonistic terms. From the point of view of enjoyment and the mitigation of boredom, a strong case can be made, as by Dewey, for a life permeated by an enlargement of the various forms of awareness, especially the capacity to solve problems and to pursue interests, such as science and art, that are open-ended in that they constantly open up new interests and problems. A life of change and challenge is advocated in which there is plenty of scope for the imagination, for the joys of mastery and the use of intelligence in shared experiences. The trouble is, however, that this defence relies on the variables of duration and fecundity in seeking satisfaction. It might have no appeal to one who relied more on the variables of certainty, intensity and propinquity. For him a life riddled with the certain if humdrum pleasures of following well-established routines with occasional plunges into more earthy and intense, if short-lived, types of satisfaction might seem more attractive. If the Dewey type of life, in which education is constitutive of personal good, were to be more decisively defended, its advocate would have, as Mill put it, to take his stand on higher ground. He would have, for instance, to appeal to additional values such as truth, or aesthetic values, or to the elimination of injustice, to which such a life might be devoted. But here again it would be difficult to decide which values, defining the higher ground, are to be deemed more important.

All such conceptions of the good life, however, might be criticised on the grounds that they are too individualistic, though this was not actually true of Dewey who stressed the value of 'shared experiences'. But even Dewey's ideal of 'growth' through problem-solving took too little account of the basic facts of our social existence. Most of the actions we perform, and activities in which we engage, arise from our 'station and its duties'. We are not free-floating atomic individuals restlessly searching for avenues of self-fulfilment. Rather there are well-trodden paths that we have to tread with others as teachers or bank clerks, fathers or mothers, secretaries or chairmen, landlords or tenants, customers or salesmen. In so far as the individual is going to 'fulfil himself', he must do so as a social being through the efficient, sincere and at times critical attention to obvious duties that confront him every day, whatever he does about more individualistic forms of satisfaction.

Such criticisms, like those of liberty from the standpoint of fairness, reflect the constant tension within democracy between the individual and social points of view. But, whichever emphasis is favoured, respect for persons surely demands that the individual should be encouraged to make something of himself, to find some role, occupation, or activity with which he can identify himself and achieve some kind of self-fulfilment. It also demands that, given the range of options open to him, his capacity for choice should be developed so that ideally he will achieve some degree of autonomy and commit himself authentically to tasks that he genuinely feels he ought to perform or to activities that he genuinely wants to pursue, as distinct from devoting himself to externally imposed duties and secondhand interests that are merely socially expected. The clash, too, between principles such as liberty and equality and the controversies about practices such as abortion and euthanasia above the level of basic moral rules will also require a similar move toward some degree of autonomy.

Authenticity and genuineness are only one facet of autonomy, which emphasise the self or *autos* aspect of it; there is also the more reflective aspect connected with the *nomos* that is to be adopted. This presupposes the weighing-up of alternatives in the effort to determine what is true, right, appropriate. With the mention of truth we arrive at the third type of value of relevance to education in a democratic society.

(c) *Truth*

The value of truth is emphasised in democracies that uphold the use of reason in social life and personal autonomy as an educational aim, though this should not be pursued completely at the expense of fraternity. Hence the salutariness of Dewey's stress on shared experiences. For truth is pursued mainly in discussion, individual reasoning being largely, as Plato put it, 'the soul's dialogue with itself'.

But in what way will the value of truth be relevant to education? Obviously it will not be just a matter of acquiring information, of attempting to memorise as many true propositions as possible; for the quickest way to do that would be to get hold of a telephone directory or an encyclopaedia and learn its contents by heart. And this might have a minimal bearing on the human condition. Nor will it usually take the form of the dedicated search for explanations in a particular area, like the scientist, or the ruthless and relentless self-examination and questioning of everything of a Socrates, though democracies encourage such relentless probings and challenges to orthodoxies of every sort. These are ways of life to which some feel called as a continuation of their education. Universities cater for such unusual people, but for the average man in his education the value of truth does not require that he become a research worker or a Socrates.

Something much more mundane is demanded. Both in his work and in his leisure-time the individual brings to his experience a stock of beliefs, attitudes and expectations. Most of these rest on authority; he has picked them up from a variety of sources. Many of them are erroneous, prejudiced and simple-minded, especially in the political realm, where evidence shows that opinions depend overwhelmingly on traditional and non-rational allegiances. One of the aims of education is to make them less so. The citizen has to be taught to look for evidence for his beliefs and to be critical of what he hears from others and acquires through the media. Of particular importance in education, as I have already suggested, will be those beliefs about the attitudes toward the human condition that will confront any man, whatever his occupation.

To expect any final truth about such matters is a chimera; but at least the individual can improve his understanding and purge his beliefs and attitudes by ridding them of error, superstition and prejudice. Also, through the development of imagination and understanding, he can come to view the human condition in a very different light. New opportunities for action may open up as his view of people, society and the natural world changes; his emotional reactions may be transformed as he gets a glimpse of the world as someone else sees it; gardening, which was a monotonous chore, may light up because of the new understanding he brings to the soil, plants and shrubs; and he may be fired by the thought of participating in the change of institutions that he had previously regarded as fixed points in his social world. Thus a mixture of intellectual probity and imaginative curiosity can gradually transform a person's outlook on nature, other people and social institutions. It should bring with it the intellectual virtues of consistency, hatred of irrelevance, clarity, precision, accuracy and a determination to look at the facts.

(d) Aesthetic and religious values
There are other values, especially aesthetic and religious ones, that are central to man's attempts to make sense of and give sense to the human condition, and hence to education, but that are not particularly distinctive of the democratic way of life. By that I mean that though religions and various forms of art flourish and are encouraged in democracies whereas they may be persecuted and severely censored in totalitarian or collectivist societies, they are possible perspectives on life that a democrat may adopt, rather than values he must accept in so far as he is committed to the types of procedure constitutive of a democratic way of life. Because, however, education demands the development of various types of awareness, individuals in a democracy should be given some form of initiation into these perspectives on the human condition in the hope that many will develop insights and sensitivities that may become of increasing significance to them. For they are persons as well as democrats, and their lives will be impoverished if they have no sense of the beauty of the world or of man's strivings to give concrete embodiment to intimations about the human condition that he cannot explicitly articulate. Similarly they will be scarcely human if they have not reflected on the place of man in the natural and historical orders. In many the contingency, creation and continuance of the world, which are beyond the power of man to comprehend, give rise to awe and wonder. The human condition is viewed in a wider perspective, under 'a certain aspect of eternity', and ways of life are generated that transcend and transform what is demanded by morality and truth. Others are content to operate within the limits of human understanding and are unmoved by reflection on the order of the world that makes such understanding possible. But both types of reaction are available only for those who have had their awareness extended in this dimension by education.

In a democracy this liberal view of the role of aesthetic and religious values in education is taken because of the importance ascribed to freedom and toleration and because of the reluctance to deprive the individual of possible ways of making something of himself provided by his cultural heritage. Having accepted the importance of aesthetic and religious values in education I will leave them on one side and refrain from exploring the specific aims they might generate. This is partly because of their complexity and the difficulty of being very determinate about them in a short space, but mainly because, as has been pointed out, they are not distinctive of the democratic way of life. To these central values and the aims of education generated by them I now return.

(4) DEMOCRATIC VALUES AND AIMS OF EDUCATION

Ever since the First World War, and the rise of totalitarian and collectivist regimes subsequent to it, it has been characteristic of democratic theories of education to postulate the self-realisation of the individual either as the aim or as the most important aim of education. Certainly this is an aim of education that needed emphasis, in spite of obscurities surrounding the type of self that was to be realised. But in view of the injustices and sense of rejection of the 'unrealised' that have been among the unintended consequences of this emphasis, it is important to return to the form of life that makes this aim possible and to place it in the context of other aims generated by the values immanent in this form of life.

(a) Interpersonal morality

Encouragement for the individual to make something of himself is feasible only in a society in which respect for persons and its offshoot, toleration, are widespread. These, together with impartiality and concern for others, are the fundamental principles of the democratic way of life, in which as much as possible is decided by discussion rather than by authorative fiat. The first priority, therefore, in a democracy is to aim at the development in its citizens of what Lawrence Kohlberg[7] calls a 'principled morality'. But, educationally speaking, the road to this is a long one. The individual has to pass from an egocentric stance toward social rules to a conventional or 'good boy' type of morality before he can emerge to a more autonomous type of morality in which fundamental principles are appealed to in dealing with dilemmas and discussing the morality of controversial practices such as abortion and the closed shop. Because, logically speaking, an individual cannot, by an appeal to principles, come to adopt a code of his own unless he has, at the conventional stage, internalised some system of rules to criticise or accept, and because achieving autonomy is very much a matter of degree, it is essential both from the individual's and from society's point of view that the individual is firmly bedded down in a basic code covering duties like those of non-injury, respect for property, whether public or private, promise-keeping, truth-telling, and so forth, at the conventional stage. For the enforcement of law cannot be omnipresent and, unless the observance of such basic duties is the general rule, no society, let alone a democratic one, could hold together for long. The problem is to teach this basic body of rules in a way that encourages the individual to move toward a more rational, principled type of morality.

This line of development from a conventional morality to a more rational one, in which some degree of autonomy is achieved, is the line of development sketched by Piaget and Kohlberg and adopted by many concerned with moral education. My viewpoint differs in two important respects.[8] First, compassion or concern for others should be given an importance equal to that accorded by Piaget and Kohlberg to the development of reason. Secondly, more emphasis should be placed on the crucial stage of conventional morality. Also, though Kohlberg, in places, makes mention of the importance of ego-strength, too little attention is paid to the virtues of the will such as perseverance, courage and integrity which are necessary for the translation of principles into practice.

(b) *Knowledge and understanding of the human condition*
Whether an individual is concerned about the plight of others or occupied with fulfilling himself in his pursuit of personal good, he must have some knowledge and understanding of the various aspects of the human condition. This utilitarian case for knowledge and understanding is reinforced by the value of truth, which suggests a non-instrumental condemnation of ignorance, error, prejudice and superstition. In what areas of life are such knowledge and understanding essential? Basically in those three spheres of being previously picked out as characterising the human condition, namely, the natural, interpersonal and sociopolitical worlds that human beings inhabit.

It goes without saying that, in an industrial society, an individual is severely handicapped if he lacks the basic skills of literacy and numeracy. For these are necessary for being at all at home in all three types of world. Urbanisation, however, has created a shield between modern man and many of the features of the natural world with which his less literate forefathers had to come to terms. But science and technology, which have been largely instrumental in creating this artificial environment, have brought in their train a host of new things to understand. So modern man, in confronting the natural world, has to understand something of gas, electricity and pollution, as well as more enduring phenomena such as fire, snow, the seasons and the properties of the soil. He must also develop a modicum of practical knowledge in dealing with them. For there are countless contingencies in an industrial society, ranging from repairs to the water system to first aid to the injured, for which expert help is not always readily available. Under our present system of schooling it tends to be only the non-academic child who gets any systematic training in such practical skills. There has been too little thought about the role of practical knowledge in education that is not part of training for a particular job.

As a member of the natural world, too, the individual must have some understanding of how his body works, of procreation, ageing and disease. The intimate connection between body and mind is being spelled out in more and more detail by physiology and brain chemistry. Awareness is subtly affected by the circulation of the blood, by glandular secretions and by the metabolic rate of the body. So not only is instruction in diet, hygiene and the avoidance of disease essential; the body must also be cared for by physical exercise of various sorts. It is rather out of fashion in physical education circles to emphasise the importance of physical fitness and the general dexterity and control of the body developed by various exercises, swimming and games. They tend to be defended because of their aesthetic features, as if footballers were like ballet dancers. Or their character-building aspects are cited. But their basic rationale in terms of care of the body is seldom stressed. Little is made, too, of the enjoyment many derive from them, which can provide a lifelong interest.

In the interpersonal world the individual has to learn to understand and adapt to others as they perform their various roles. But he also has to discern the individual at the centre of these socially expected routines with all his inner motives, aspirations and idiosyncratic perspectives on the world. Such understanding is not easy to achieve, yet there are psychiatrists who argue that many of the milder forms of mental illness can be traced back to systematic misperceptions and misunderstandings of ourselves and others, and to consequent failures to form satisfactory relationships. The positive value of understanding others in co-operative projects, community life and forming friendships is obvious enough. Also, interpersonal morality presupposes an accurate assessment of motives and intentions if moral judgements are to be realistically based. This form of understanding is central to the education of the emotions, which is one of the most sadly neglected spheres of education.

In the sociopolitical sphere much is demanded of a citizen of a democratic state. He must have a general knowledge of how the political system works, and be sensitive to the social and economic conditions that it has to shape and by which it is shaped. He must be familiar enough with current affairs to criticise policies constructively and to make up his own mind which way to cast his vote. Ideally, too, he should possess the social skills necessary to participate in public affairs at least at the local level.

This, of course, is only a rough and sketchy indication of the types of knowledge and understanding that anyone in a democratic society should possess in order to participate in this form of life, and that is also required by the demands of truth that democracy endorses. But it can, of course, given curiosity, the development of imagination and, perhaps, what Simone Weil calls 'a love of the world' be extended infinitely by study of the natural sciences, geography, history, psychology, literature and the social sciences. Experience of people, places and institutions can gradually be transformed by the new conceptual frameworks in which they are located.

It might, however, be argued that this is little more than a refurbished version of Dewey's approach to education – that learning should be related to the solution of some current practical or social problem and that 'subjects' should be taught only on this condition. This, in my view, is too narrow a way of formulating the relevance to the human condition that I take to be the hallmark of the type of learning that we call education. To start with I am suggesting that people should be introduced to knowledge about matters that will predictably be of some significance to them at some time in their lives as persons; I am not saying that they should be introduced to it only when confronted by a practical problem to which it is relevant. One of the hallmarks of a good teacher is to stimulate new interests, not just rely on existing ones.

Secondly, much of the knowledge of the human condition is not of immediate practical use; rather it transforms a person's conception of the general context in which life has to be lived. The Copernican theory, which shattered the belief that the earth was the centre of the solar system, was of profound emotional significance to human beings; this was far more important than the marginal improvements it permitted in navigation. Similarly, the emotional significance of the theory of evolution was of far more significance to the average man than its practical outcomes, and Freud's claim that the thought and conduct of the grown man are influenced by unconscious infantile wishes is of more significance because of its transformation of man's conception of himself than because of its faltering and often fruitless practical outcomes in therapy. Much of education is concerned not with answering practical problems but with mapping the contours of the general conditions within which such problems arise.

Thirdly, many problems are wrongly so called; for a problem is something that, in principle, admits of a solution. Many situations with which the individual will have to deal cannot be so optimistically described. They are predicaments that he somehow has to learn to live with, such as the inevitability of death, the birth of a badly deformed child, a heart attack or unexpected redundancy in middle age. Understanding and the reorientation of attitudes can do something to help the individual to live with such predicaments, though, as was argued before in discussing happiness, it is optimistic to expect too much. But they cannot be 'fixed up' by technology.

Finally, the case for knowledge and understanding does not rest purely on their relevance to practical and social problems and their emotional significance to anyone in trying to discern the contours of the human condition. There is also truth, which is conceptually connected with knowledge, and a value in its own right. By that I mean that, other things being equal, being deluded, in error, or prejudiced are just bad states of mind to be in. For belief is the state of mind appropriate to what is true; and though true beliefs usually help us to further our practical purposes, their value does not derive from this source alone. Truth just matters, irrespective of its payoff.

(c) *The self-fulfilment of the individual*
What is to be made of the traditional aim of democratic education – the growth, self-realisation, or self-actualisation of the individual? There is an initial obscurity about it, for some theorists have a definite view of the sort of self that ought to be realised, whereas others regard it as a very individual matter. Carl Rogers, for instance, finds that, given appropriate circumstances, individuals move towards genuineness, acceptance of self, openness to others and self-direction. But the qualities characterising Roger's 'self' are almost identical with those advocated as values immanent in his client-centred therapy; it seems improbable that they are the products of some spontaneous unfolding of dormant potentialities. Those, on the other hand, who stress individuality and the many avenues open to the individual in his search for self-fulfilment must rule out certain avenues that are manifestly immoral and stress the development of autonomy without which the individual cannot choose which avenues to explore. And these requirements presuppose a lengthy period of moral education dealt with in the first aim, and the development of a widely informed imagination dealt with in the second aim.

These brief reflections suggest that self-realisation involves authentic commitment by the individual to modes of conduct, beliefs, attitudes and activities made available to him by the types of learning falling under the first two aims of education. It is an offshoot of these two basic aims. It has, however, two dangers. The first is that it may encourage too self-conscious a search for avenues of fulfilment. Those who achieve some kind of self-fulfilment are usually absorbed in various activities and duties with which they identify themselves wholeheartedly without much thought of realising themselves. Secondly, like the old quest for individual salvation, it may degenerate into a lonely quest at the expense of fraternity and a sense of community. Dewey, in his emphasis on shared experiences, was acutely aware of this too individualistic perversion of this democratic aim. So is Rogers with his stress on personal relationships as the essential context for the development of the self. Given these qualifications and caveats, a place must surely be made, grounded on respect for persons, for the self-fulfilment of the individual as an aim of education. Opportunities should be provided for all to participate in activities and pursuits and to undertake responsibilities with which they can identify themselves and attain some kind of mastery. These may be shared experiences such as science, social reform, or sports, or more individual activities such as cooking, gardening, or astronomy. If there is some kind of identification of the individual with the pursuit or duty, it will give the individual an introduction to non-alienated learning. It will do something to generate self-respect, which is central both to character and to motivation, and will bring with it virtues of the will, especially attention, concentration and perseverance, to which, in my opinion, too little attention is paid in our present educational system.

(d) Preparation for work?

I have made the point that, in democracies, there is a constant tension between the pursuit of personal and public good and that this manifests itself in the types of emphasis that emerge as educational aims. One criticism that is current at the moment, of the emphasis on individual self-fulfilment, is that it has been to the detriment of the economy. Insufficient attention is being paid to preparing the citizen for an occupation. There is nothing specifically democratic about this aim, but as it is *also* argued for as an obvious avenue of self-fulfilment for the individual, and hence an offshoot of the aim, it is worth ending with a few brief comments about it. These comments may be superfluous in ten years' time; for if technological change continues in its present direction, the demand may well be that education should do more to prepare people for leisure. The present demand is often misleadingly expressed in terms of preparation for work; for leisure time activities like making cupboards, playing the violin and growing roses involve work just as much as do tool-making, scientific research, bricklaying and running a school. So if what is really meant is 'work', this has already been covered by aims *b* and *c*.

Manifestly, however, people who stress the importance of preparation for work[9] are not talking about work but about jobs or occupations. And many jobs do not involve work but what Hannah Arendt called 'labour'.[10] This distinction is difficult to demarcate briefly, but roughly it is between activities in which the individual employs some kind of skill to create a relatively durable product that he can see to be the result of his own efforts, and those in which he employs little skill in contributing to some process whose end-product he may never see, or for which he feels little responsibility, or in which what he helps to create is more or less immediately consumed or destroyed. The rewards of labour are extrinsic. The lavatory attendant goes through endless routines of changing towels and toilet rolls, and sweeping the floor, with thoughts in his head about the pay packet at the end of the week. Work, on the other hand, though it may have extrinsic payoffs, is done basically for the enjoyments intrinsic to it. Thus labour involves what Marx called 'alienation'; the individual cannot identify himself with what he is doing. He is at home when he is not labouring, and when he is labouring he is not at home.

Preparation for jobs, therefore, raises complex questions. In so far as a job involves some specific sort of work, there is no reason why the individual should not opt for preparation for it at school if it is likely to provide a concrete motivational focus for his education as well as an aid to the economy. But this is to be encouraged only on two conditions. First, it should not just be narrow training. It should also serve as a way into the understanding of principles of more general application and as a focus for more general matters of human concern. Secondly, it should not take place too early because of the danger of prematurely determining an individual's life-chances. It might be argued, too, that a greater use of day-release would be a better way of catering for this demand than a widespread attempt to bring the factory and office into the school, especially as techniques in industry change so rapidly.

But what is to be said about preparing people for labour? For it surely is not the business of education to prepare pupils to tolerate boredom and frustration, even though this is what some schools unwittingly do by the alienation of pupils from the learning to which they are exposed. Yet there are countless jobs in an industrial society that fall into the category of labour, for which little in the way of special preparation is required. This widespread problem is surely one for politicians, unions and employers to tackle – for example, by rearranging labour so that more of it approximates to work, by worker-participation schemes, and by more flexible hours that permit employees to plan their day so that more activities involving work can be fitted in off the job. Education can, of course, improve the quality of personal relationships of those who labour; it can encourage a spirit of service to the community, equip people for more constructive use of their leisure, and encourage a sense of outrage at depersonalising conditions of employment. It can, too, discourage the tendency to identify a person with the job that perforce he or she may have to perform. But it cannot transform labour into work and can only gradually contribute to changing a society that tolerates such widespread alienation. Unfortunately the influence is too often the other way round. For in many schools mindless rote learning in order to pass examinations mirrors the alienated labour of the factory floor.

CONCLUSION

This brief catalogue of aims may sound a bit mundane and unexciting. How much more inspiring it would be to proclaim with Dewey that 'education is growth' or with Whitehead that it is 'the art of the utilisation of knowledge' or with Hegel that 'education is the art of making man ethical'. But all such concepts of education are contestable, for what has happened is that an aim of education has been taken as *the* aim and incorporated into the concept of 'education'. It is easy to see how this happens, for education is a teleological type of concept in that it indicates processes of learning directed towards some end. Particular ends that require emphasis can then be singled out to the exclusion of other possible ones and the result is a stipulative definition.

I have tried to avoid this by sketching what I take to be incontestable about education and then articulating some major aims that could give direction to it. In order to avoid the charge of arbitrariness, I have tried to show the values from which such aims can be derived. They are, of course, eminently contestable because, first, I have confined myself to democratic values; secondly, my concept of democracy is contestable; and thirdly, I have dealt only briefly with aesthetic and religious values as not being particularly distinctive of democracy. Many might regard this brevity as banal. Finally, though probably all democrats would agree about the importance of morality, and truth, there could be disputes about my interpretation of these values and what aspects of them should be emphasised as aims of education.

Thus, though the aims I have suggested are contestable, they are not just my personal preference, for they have been presented as emphases within a public form of life. Indeed I have followed Plato's contention that there is a fit between a type of state and a type of man. My account, however, of both the democratic state and the democratic man differs radically from Plato's. There is, of course, a general similarity in that, on both accounts, the development of reason occupies a central place in education. But whereas for Plato this is represented as a process by means of which a few arrive at an authoritative vision of the Good, both an agreed end-point and the existence of such an elite are denied by the democrat. Instead stress is placed on the social principles presupposed by the use of reason in social and personal life and the intellectual virtues implicit in the elimination of prejudice, superstition and error. Democracy is concerned more with principles for proceeding than with a determinate destination and aims of education in a democracy should emphasise the qualities of mind essential for such a shared journey.

REFERENCES: CHAPTER 3

1 Gallie, W.B., 'Essentially contested concepts', *Proceedings of the Aristotelian Society,* vol. 56, 1955–6, and Hartnell, A. and Naish, M., *Theory and Practice of Education,* Vol. 1 (London: Heinemann, 1976), pp. 79–94.
2 Stevenson, C., 'Persuasive definitions', *Mind,* 1938.
3 See Langford, G.H., and O'Connor, D.J., *New Essays in the Philosophy of Education* (London: Routledge & Kegan Paul, 1973).
4 Bereiter, C., *Must We Educate?* (Englewood Cliffs, NJ: Prentice-Hall, 1973).
5 Downie, R.S., Telfer, E., and Loudfoot, E.M., *Education and Personal Relationships* (London: Methuen, 1974).
6 Peters, R.S., *Ethics and Education* (London: Allen & Unwin, 1965), ch. 11.
7 Kohlberg, L., 'From is to ought', in Mischel, T. (ed), *Cognitive Development and Epistemology* (New York: Academic Press, 1971).
8 See Peters, R.S., 'The place of Kohlberg's theory in moral education', *Journal of Moral Education,* vol. 7, no. 3, May 1978.
9 See, for example, Warnock, M., *Schools of Thought* (London: Faber, 1977), ch. 4, pp. 143–51.
10 See Arendt, H., *The Human Condition* (Chicago: University of Chicago Press, 1958), chs, 3, 4.

Part Two
Tradition and Progressivism

Chapter 4

Herbert Spencer's Scientific Progressivism

INTRODUCTION

What is the point in resurrecting the works of an educator who is so seldom read? In part curiosity; for Spencer's *Essays on Education* were highly influential at the time when he wrote.* After a brief period of popularity in England and the USA, they passed out of favour more or less into oblivion. And none of the commentators can adequately explain this rather strange phenomenon.[1] It is interesting, therefore, to peruse his works to see if they contain anything of permanent as distinct from purely contemporary significance.

The second reason is that Spencer was a populariser with a great gift for synthesis. He was a prophet both of evolution and of 'natural education'. Though he claimed that he had never read Rousseau, he was obviously familiar with his ideas, and his essay on 'Intellectual education' was in part a critique of Pestalozzi. One would hope to find in Spencer, therefore, an orderly and measured exposition of the tenets of 'natural education' which one does not find in his less coherent predecessors.

Finally, with modern discussion centring on the core curriculum, the title of his most famous essay, 'What knowledge is of most worth?' has a modern ring to it. To a modern reader it may not quite satisfy the promise of its title because of Spencer's conviction of the omnipresence of science. But his treatment of the question is interesting and provocative, and his plea for the importance of scientific education is particularly pertinent at the present time.

---

*They were composed separately for magazines: 'What knowledge is of most worth?' in the *Westminster Review* in 1859, 'Intellectual education' in the *North British Review* in 1854 and 'Moral education' and 'Physical education' in the *British Quarterly Review* in 1858 and 1859. They were put together in a book in 1861. He also dealt with the political aspects of education: for example, the rights of children and state provision of education, in his *Social Statics* in 1851.

(1) SPENCER'S OVERALL END

Reading Spencer's *Essays on Education* is a strange experience; for he did not, like most educators, write as a participant in the enterprise – indeed he was never a teacher or father. Rather he wrote as a spectator, from an external-descriptive point of view. He saw man, as part of Nature, moving towards an evolutionary end. This was the extremely individualistic one of 'complete living' or happiness for every individual. Certain procedures in schools and child-rearing he deemed counter-productive in relation to this end, unnatural impositions of man's uninstructed will. The thrust of his *Essays* is to single out types of knowledge and practices that are consonant with, and to condemn those which are contrary to, the tendencies of Nature. Thus parents and teachers should be 'ministers and interpreters of Nature'.[2] To fulfil this role properly they must acquaint themselves with the relevant sciences which reveal the laws of Nature's operations.

This evolutionary end gave coherence to Spencer's proposals but its status was shrouded in a convenient ambiguity. To start with, why should it be thought of as a desirable end? For evolution, which was a scientific theory, conferred no moral merit on any of its outcomes. Henry Sidgwick was to raise this difficulty in his critique of Spencer's later *The Data of Ethics*.[3] There is also the indeterminate status, as in other evolutionary theories such as Marxism, of informed human intervention. This occurs not just at the individual level of the 'adjustment of acts to ends', when the teacher makes his conduct more or less in conformity with Nature; it occurs, too, at the state level at which Spencer vigorously opposed state intervention in education as being an impediment to the evolutionary end of 'complete living'. What would he have made of the status of this end had he known that state education would become normal practice and that a large portion of mankind would devote themselves to the collectivist end of citizenship in a classless society? Spencer, however, was an optimist imbued with the scientific spirit of the times and with a firm belief in progress under conditions of *laissez-faire*. So he stated his ethical convictions as if they were scientific tendencies and made his educational proposals fit into this general framework.

Spencer might have been wise to confine himself to saying that 'complete living' is the end of education; for that is vague and high-sounding enough to fulfil this sort of role and he later spelled out in some detail what he thought to be involved in it. But he was unwise enough to link this end with happiness, which is a more specific notion that is much more questionable as a feasible end of education. This is not the place to query the status of happiness as the, or an, end of life or to raise doubts about whether other values such as truth and justice can plausibly be defended as dependent upon it. The difficulty that concerns us is that of making it the end of education.[4]

(2) THE CONTENT OF EDUCATION

Spencer's account of the content of education was highly individualistic, not to say self-centred. He declared flatly 'to prepare us for complete living is the function which education has to perform'[5] and listed the activities which he deemed conducive to this individual end. There are firstly activities which directly minister to self-preservation. Nature has provided man with an instinctive equipment to safeguard him; but this needs to be supplemented by a knowledge of physiological laws that are known to promote health and prevent disease.

Secondly, there are activities which indirectly contribute to self-preservation by facilitating the gaining of a livelihood. So important are they that many consider them to be the chief end of education. For most such activities will consist in the production, preparation and exchange of commodities. Efficiency will depend upon adequate acquaintance with the sciences that underlie them, whether it be the physical sciences for those working in docks or engineering or biology for the farmer. Social science is useful to understand the entangled activities of commerce and, with the coming of the joint-stock company, may even be of use in making wise investments! This type of knowledge is left out of the curricula of most schools; yet industry would come to a halt were it not for the acquisition of it after schooling has finished. It is picked up in 'nooks and corners: while the ordained agencies for teaching have been mumbling little else but dead formulas'.[6]

Thirdly, there is the rearing and disciplining of children, for which no provision is made on the curriculum of schools. Indeed he says that a puzzled antiquary of the future, perusing current curricula and examinations, would conclude that the curriculum had been devised for celibates! The fate of future generations is left to the chances of unreasoning custom, impulse and fancy to which are added the suggestions of ignorant nurses and the prejudiced counsel of grandmothers. Enormous harm is done to children as a result – perhaps early death or feeble constitutions. And moral training is as haphazard as physical, dependent upon whims of parents, threats and bribes, instead of on acquaintance with physiology and the elementary truths of psychology. Ignorance of the laws governing the phenomena of intelligence is equally widespread. Symbols are substituted for observation and experiment and the laws of mental development are disregarded in the teaching of abstractions and the vicious practice of rote learning. The child is encouraged to become a mere passive recipient of other people's ideas, not an active inquirer or self-instructor. 'What remains is mostly inert – the art of applying knowledge not having been cultivated.'[7]

The fourth sphere of knowledge is that relating to citizenship. This is not overlooked because it is thought that history contributes to it.

Unfortunately the wrong sort of history is taught – a recital of battles and court intrigues. It should be replaced by the more relevant study of descriptive sociology, though this will not provide satisfactory understanding unless it is underpinned by the sciences of biology and psychology. For society is made up of individuals and all that is done in society is done by the combined action of individuals. Therefore in individual actions only can be found the solutions of social phenomena, and psychology is the science in which they are studied.

The final division of human life consists in the relaxations and amusements which are enjoyed in leisure-time. As working conditions improve these will be of increasing importance. Aesthetic culture is greatly conducive to human happiness, but is not fundamental to it as are the activities previously considered. For they make individual and social life possible and are thus presupposed by aesthetic pursuits. The latter are the efflorescence of civilised life. Educational systems are apt to neglect the plant for the sake of the flower in the attention which they give to them. Spencer then proceeded to argue the improbable thesis that the highest art of every kind is based on science. Sculptors and painters have to be cognisant with the laws of the phenomena which they represent – with anatomy, for instance. Music and poetry might seem exceptions to this. But they are not; for they are the expressions of feeling and as such fall under that branch of psychology which deals with the laws of nervous action!

So Spencer, in his account of the content of education, did two things. First, he charted the areas which should be studied in order of importance to self-preservation. Secondly, he claimed that 'the knowledge that is of most worth' in all these areas was science. These two aspects of his undertaking need to be considered separately. For it would be unkind to dismiss him out of hand because he thought that the laws of nervous reaction (*sic*) could explain one of Shakespeare's sonnets.

(a) *Educational priorities*

Rousseau said of Emile 'Life is the trade that I would teach him' and Spencer commendably followed him in seeing that education, as distinct from training, is the kind of learning that equips a person *qua* person to face the predictable contingencies of the human condition as distinct from preparing him purely for some specific skill or role. But his view of the human condition, and hence of his catalogue of aids to 'complete living', was warped by the narrowness of his conception of the end of life. He provided guides to the atomic individual in his lonely quest for a demythologised form of personal salvation, not advice and encouragement to a fellow-sufferer in a shared predicament. Even his attitude to citizenship was one of judicious appraisal of a survival kit; it was not a series of suggestions about how the individual could co-operate and contribute to the common good.

Understandably, therefore, the most conspicuous absentee from his list of 'knowledge that is of most worth' is understanding of others and of oneself – in many ways one of the most important and difficult forms of knowledge to acquire. Yet its indispensability cannot be gainsaid. For human beings, willy-nilly, share a social form of life and one of the first things they have to learn is to interpret and respond to the actions and gestures of others. Positively, the value of such knowledge in day-to-day relationships, in co-operation and in friendship is obvious enough. But there is no mention of this sort of knowledge in Spencer's account. He stresses the importance of the psychological understanding of children by parents and teachers, but does not deal with the general sort of knowledge involved. No doubt he would have said that it is a branch of psychology! But his highly individualistic approach precluded any explicit treatment of it.

Much understanding of others comes from sensitivity to their motives. And it is interesting that the names of most motives such as pride, envy, jealousy, benevolence, ambition and lust are also the names of virtues and vices. This brings us to another lacuna in Spencer's account. Parents are exhorted to master the laws of cause and effect in order to conduct their children's moral training, but nothing is said of their own consciousness of right and wrong. Given his poor opinion of parents he cannot have believed that they themselves had mastered the tendencies of actions to promote happiness or misery, which on his view would have provided them with such a consciousness. There is also J. S. Mill's point that there is a place for moral instruction because the experience of the race had provided 'secondary principles', such as that promises ought to be kept, which were reliable guides. So the individual did not always have to do his own moral homework. Indeed, Spencer's own individualism, with its uncompromising belief in the freedom of the individual to pursue his own happiness, presupposed toleration and respect for persons as moral principles. For his scheme of education to be viable, should he not have insisted that teachers and parents alike had rock-like convictions about the importance of these principles? For they alone could provide the framework within which his guides to 'complete living' could operate. For him this sort of knowledge should have been of supreme worth; for he was opposed to the state providing the necessary framework.

These two criticisms can be summed up by saying that Spencer's evolutionary approach and his advocacy of following Nature made man appear like a self-contained organism in a social environment that is alien to him. If teachers and parents impart what is purely social, they are introducing an undesirable element of artifice. Even cultural products such as music and poetry are superimpositions on the individual's nervous reactions.

Spencer had a balanced view of vocational education. He accorded it importance but not over-riding importance and insisted that it must be mounted on a firm theoretical base. But he understandably passed by two problems that plague discussions of relating education to occupation. First of all, his examples are all of activities such as engineering and farming which require skill and judgement and which have a solid scientific base. He did not foresee the problem of mass education in an industrial society in which the majority are destined for jobs requiring little skill and judgement and for which practically no training – scientific or otherwise – is required. Secondly, he gives no warning of the dangers of early specialisation which may prematurely determine a person's life-chances.

Perhaps the most barbarous of all Spencer's suggestions was that literature, poetry, art, music, and so on, are to be viewed just as leisure-time pursuits. No doubt this is one of their important functions and Spencer was prophetic in discerning their increasing importance as such with the shortening of the working day. But to view them only under this aspect is grotesque; for the value of a literary or artistic education is not to be estimated just in terms of the books which an individual continues to read or the art galleries which he visits. The question is what such studies have done to his perceptions, sensitivities and imagination. It may be too strong to call the aesthetic a form of knowledge, but certainly activities of this type provide perspectives on the human situation which are complementary to the abstractions of the sciences. And many would argue that a man is not 'living completely' if he lacks these perspectives, whatever he does in his leisure-time.

(b) Spencer's scientism

There is no doubt that Spencer had a strong case in his plea for science. For science, on which the nation's industrial and commercial future depended, was widely neglected by universities and public schools in favour of classical and literary studies. It flourished in mechanics institutes and other 'nooks and corners' of the educational system. His plea is almost as pertinent today with the constant cry for more scientists and mathematicians in the schools and higher education. The facilities are there, as they were not in Spencer's day, but the young have not become disciples of Spencer.

Spencer, however, spoilt his case by overstating it. It was innocuous enough to suggest that mothers, in bringing up their children, could do with a knowledge of physiology and of the 'elementary truths' of psychology, although the world still waits to know what these truths are. On the place of physics and mechanics in industrial life, he was, too, on safe ground; for he had trained as an engineer and worked for two short spells on the railways. But in his suggestion that painting was also scientific, because it required a mastery of anatomy, his enthusiasm outran his judgement. Even granted the representational view of art which he presupposed, *The Last Supper* does not become scientific because Leonardo knew some anatomy, any more than the construction of a dam becomes a mathematical work because the engineers know some mathematics. It was suprising that Spencer did not stress rather than just mention an elementary knowledge of logic; for all forms of thought employ the basic principles of logic. They are much more essential to scientific thinking than science is to the work of the artist. The point is to look at the character of the questions to which an answer is sought, or of the experiences which are being embodied in some medium. Artists may make use of some science here and there, but their predominating purpose is not to answer scientific questions.

Spencer's suggestion that the wrong sort of history should be replaced by descriptive sociology seems inappropriate; for why not replace it by a more appropriate sort of history focused on contemporary problems and concerns? History makes uses of generalisations from sociology and economics but is not itself a generalising science. It is concerned with particular actions that happened and why. Spencer put his head into a hornet's nest of twentieth-century controversy about the autonomy of sociology by his further suggestion that sociological phenomena could be explained in psychological terms. His suggestion, too, that music was basically scientific because it was an expression of feeling, to be explained in terms of the laws of nervous reaction, was another eccentric barbarism.

In substituting science for other modes of experience Spencer had unbounded faith in psychology – a faith that looks rather pathetic after over a hundred years of contending schools and unresolved controversies. William James's words nearly a hundred years ago still have some point: 'not a single law in the sense which physics shows us laws, not a single proposition from which any consequences can be causally deduced . . . This is no science, it is only the hope of a science.'[8] Spencer wrote his own ambitious *Principles of Psychology* in 1855 in which he achieved fame for the definition of life as 'the continuous adjustment of internal relations to external relations'. Psychology deals with the processes through which the conscious organism maintains itself in its environment, mediating the transition from biology to sociology. But though his synthetic endeavours as a systematiser were important, the actual content of his psychology was little improvement on traditional associationism, with the life of mind being brought under the general rubric of a correlation between inner and outer activities. There was little in this synthesis of current theories that could provide explanation of the phenomena which he claimed could be explained by psychology. It was more important as a programme than as a performance.[9]

(*c*) *Science as mental discipline*

Having dealt with the worth of the content of science, Spencer then turned to its value as a mental discipline. This section has an archaic ring about it as the mind is no longer regarded as composed of various faculties such as 'judgement' that can be trained in a general sort of way by specific studies. It could well be, for instance, that historical studies contribute to shrewd judgements about current events. But whether or not a historian will be a better judge of what his friends or colleagues are likely to do in a given situation is a further question. It raises the much-disputed question of the transfer of training.

Spencer first of all deployed a general teleological type of argument, claiming that it would be against the economy of Nature if one kind of culture was needed for giving information and another as a mental gymnastic. He supported this profession of evolutionary faith with the evidence of memory and judgement, both of which are trained by science. He then suggested that science is a better moral discipline than, for instance, languages; for in languages things are either right or wrong and the appeal must be made to authority to decide. Science, on the other hand, does not so depend upon authority. It appeals to the individual reason of the inquirer. This argument has an attractive plausibility about it. But it has two flaws in it apart from the general one of depending not upon an examination of the morals of scientists and linguists but upon a presumed fit between their training and their morals. The first flaw is that there is no guarantee that the scientist's reliance on individual reason extends beyond his laboratory. Many scientists have been loyal, uncritical members of collectivist parties. Secondly, as Kuhn argued, there are periods of 'normal science' when some paradigm is widely accepted and most scientists are occupied in filling in the details. The scope for 'individual reason' is much more limited. At the time when Spencer was writing independence of mind and 'individual reason' were very much to the fore; for this was a revolutionary period of science with the battle between science and religion gathering momentum. It was not a period when collective reason was more to the fore.

Spencer ended his essay by pointing out that science also provides religious culture; for it is only to superstition, not to essential religion, that it is hostile. Indeed he said that 'devotion to science is a tacit worship'.[10] It generates a profound respect for the uniformities that things disclose. In conforming, man sees that the process of things is towards a greater perfection and a higher happiness. Science alone, too, gives a true conception of ourselves and our relation to the mysteries of existence. It brings home to us the littleness of human intelligence in the face of that which transcends intelligence. Maybe – but more effectively than the psalms, the poems of John Donne or Tolstoy's *War and Peace*?

(*d*) *Science and the worth of knowledge*
Spencer's technique for establishing the supreme worth of science was most ingenious, if far-fetched. It consisted in showing that all other contenders were either forms of science or pastimes with a scientific substructure. In discussing his claim a similar sort of move might have to be made with the aesthetic and religious realms; for it might be cogently argued that it is too strong to say that knowledge is available in these spheres. This would raise the question of the importance of knowledge as distinct from the perspectives provided from these spheres and it would be difficult to decide by what criteria such a dispute could be settled. Is appreciation of the *Mona Lisa* of more 'worth' than Ohm's Law? Indeed, if one wanted to get really tough one might say that in science itself we do not have knowledge but well-confirmed conjectures. A really tight sense of 'knowledge' might confine us to logic and pure mathematics. For our purposes, however, it will serve to count history, science and morality as knowledge. For in these spheres there are established bodies of belief and more or less agreed procedures for discussing them.

Leaving aside Spencer's ingenious way of answering his question, what is to be made of his substantive claim? He was surely right in claiming that science is of great worth to mankind and should be a compulsory part of the curriculum. The reason is that education is concerned with the development of a person *qua* person and should fit the individual to understand and to be at home in the various spheres of the human condition that are to be predictably encountered – natural, interpersonal, socioeconomic and political. Various forms of science, together with some history, are indispensable for this. Science, too, is indispensable in adapting nature, it is to be hoped in not too philistine a manner, to human needs and purposes. And, as Spencer stressed, it underlies industry, trade and commerce.

Equally indispensable, however, is the development of the moral consciousness of the individual. Spencer argued that science encourages morality because of its rejection of authority and reliance on individual reason. But in his usual individualistic way he ignored the fact that science is a social activity dependent on moral virtues like truthfulness, not cheating, co-operation, respect for the point of view of others and impartiality. Furthermore the end which he envisaged for education, that of 'complete living' for the individual, would only be possible in a society which encouraged tolerance of individual attempts to attain this evolutionary end. So moral understanding and sensitivity would be at least of equal worth to science. So too would the under-standing of others which is so closely intertwined with morality. Spencer might have claimed that this is a branch of his ubiquitous psychology. But others might argue that more insight in this sphere can be gleaned from reading George Eliot, Tolstoy and Henry James than from delving into psychology text books.

There is a further way in which the moral consciousness of the individual interpenetrates the scientific. With his belief in evolutionary progress Spencer hoped that science would be used for beneficent purposes. He lived before Belsen and Hiroshima. But a responsible scientist cannot dissociate himself from the uses to which his discoveries are put. So the 'individual reason' of the scientist is a myth. He is ringed round by the moral norms constitutive of scientific discussion. On the other hand his conscience may call a halt to experiments that are likely to entail suffering or the infringements of the rights of others.

And yet, if science cannot operate in a moral vacuum, neither can morality be impervious to scientific findings. One does not have to be a utilitarian to argue that the consequences of actions and social practices are, at times, relevant to their morality. The sciences come on the scene in helping to estimate them. So both science and morality would have worth in their own right and as supporting each other. In the centre of the scene, also, would be the understanding of others which is indispensable for life generally as well as for both morality and science. History would fall into this category; for it is basically an attempt to reconstruct the actions and rethink the thoughts of dead men.

To ask, therefore, whether science has most worth is an unanswerable question. Apart from the difficulty of the criterion by reference to which the question might be answered, once Spencer's extremely individualistic end is abandoned, there is the interlocking character of the activities which has been demonstrated. Science, as an activity, is supported by moral norms and scientists have a moral responsibility in relation to their findings. They have to understand each other and make use of historical evidence in putting forward some of their conjectures. Historians similarly make use of scientific generalisations. Morality, on the other hand, makes use of scientific findings and can make no responsible judgements on others without some attempt to understand them.

(3) THE METHODS OF EDUCATION

There is not a great deal to be said about Spencer's essay on 'Intellectual education' because most of it had been said before by Rousseau and Pestalozzi. Spencer merely marshalled familiar doctrines in a more coherent form with some comments on the apparent failure of some of Pestalozzi's doctrines in practice.

After some perceptive generalities about the relationship between education and the general state of the country, Spencer opened with an attack against the rote learning of rules; the important thing is to lead the child to a grasp of principles. Truths must be presented in the concrete by reliance on experiment and discovery. But above all learning must be pleasurable. The rise of appetite for any kind of information implies that the unfolding mind has become fit to assimilate it. Ascetism is disappearing out of education as it is out of life. The common characteristic of these new methods is their increasing conformity to the methods of Nature, for instance the early emphasis on the senses, on oral and experimental methods instead of on rote learning. Above all the attempt to present knowledge attractively follows Nature's behests and adjusts our proceedings to the laws of life. Why, then, have a curriculum? Why not leave children solely to the discipline of Nature? Because of the long process of maturation of human beings. This slow development of organs requires parents and teachers to act as facilitators of the process of evolution until the stage of independence is reached – whenever that is!

Spencer then discussed possible reasons why Pestalozzi's system had failed, or at least fallen short of its promise. One of his major explanations was that Pestalozzi proceeded by intuition; he was not a systematic thinker and had a limited knowledge of the principles in accordance with which the faculties unfold. Spencer proceeded to provide these, thinking that he was enunciating psychological laws of the mind – for example, simple must precede complex, indefinite must precede definite, concrete must precede abstract, empirical must precede rational, and so on. He went on to reiterate Rousseau's polemic against telling children things instead of letting them find out things for themselves, and, like Rousseau, advocated the discipline of Nature through careful ministration.

Spencer then returned to his theme of the importance of pleasurable learning in children, claiming that the child's intellectual instincts are more trustworthy than our reasoning. He admitted, however, that some of the higher mental powers, exercised only by a few, may have to be brought into play by ulterior motives. Does Nature fail to operate, then, when a few fail to master the earlier steps? Or is not Nature also operating when a child writes a story to please his teacher or does his homework to placate his parents? Do not 'ulterior motives' operate throughout education and, though they may not be as desirable as pleasurable excitement with what has to be learned, are they not 'natural'? Indeed what is more 'natural' than a child's desire for approval?

Spencer's insistence that learning must be pleasant, which is meant to follow 'Nature's behest', is understandable as a reaction against rote learning and a lot of boring instruction, but is a piece of romantic exaggeration as a positive doctrine. Firstly, Spencer himself, in his later doctrine of 'natural consequences', stressed that children learn much from the pain that attends their own wrong-doing. The same holds in the intellectual sphere. The disappointment of making mistakes is one form of learning, however much it is condemned by Skinnerians. Secondly, if Spencer meant merely that children should want to learn what they have to learn, few would deny the desirability of such an ideal situation. But, as Whitehead later pointed out, the stage of romance is followed by the stage of precision. What is initially attractive soon begins to make demands for precision, accuracy and standards. The problem is often one of sustaining pleasurable interest rather than of arousing it. Also if children want some long-term end sufficiently strongly they will often grind away at learning which they may find unpleasant in order to achieve it. This case is unlike that of an 'ulterior end', in which the reward such as approval may be quite disconnected from the learning. I have in mind cases where the learning is tightly related to the end – for example, a boy learning to file and to use a mill who wants to become a tool-maker.

The basic unreality underlying Spencer's whole picture of natural pleasurable learning is his organic as distinct from social conception of man. He viewed the child as an organism evolving towards a predetermined end, guided in his reactions to Nature by the ministrations of external agents such as parents and teachers. He lacked the vision of Marx who saw that the social existence of man largely determines his consciousness. There may, for instance, be some innate curiosity in every child. But whether this is encouraged or damped down depends very much on his home and the social attitudes there prevalent. If a middle-class child comes to school keen to learn, and finds learning pleasant, it is not just Nature working through him as Spencer thought. It is also his home and class-background. Children do not always find some things 'naturally' pleasant and other things unpleasant. Their view of them is determined by their peers, parents – even teachers. This is not to say, of course, that there are no individual preferences and idiosyncracies. That would be as absurd as Spencer's doctrine. But it is to say that the concept of the individual must be understood as a meeting-place and mirroring from a particular standpoint of countless social influences. The individual is not entirely constituted by such influences; for he or she brings to them an active, selective ordering which is determined in part by innate constitution. But they provide the perspectives out of which the individual gradually makes himself.

There is also the converse point that children may find things pleasant which it is not desirable to learn – for example, making fires. That Nature does not necessarily discipline them not to do such things is admitted by Spencer when he argues that, because of the long process of maturation of human beings, parents and teachers must for a long time act as facilitators of Nature. In other words, until 'independence' is reached, they must decide which forms of learning are desirable and which not. Once this is admitted the role of Nature becomes much more subordinate to that of human decision, as is obvious enough if one is not concerned, like Spencer, to fit education into an evolutionary form of development.

In arguing for the inadequacy of Nature to do the whole job of education Spencer drew attention to the importance of language, which is essential for knowledge, and which is acquired from others. But he did not develop this crucial point about man as a social being. For in learning a language a child departs from his organic self-sufficiency. He begins to encounter a world structured through the concepts of his community, which embodies the community's accumulated experience and wisdom. It is into this that the child has to be initiated and within this that he has to learn to make something of himself. Of course any wise teacher will use his interests and what he finds pleasant to introduce him to various modes of experience so that, hopefully, he can eventually strike out on his own. But he will not let what is interesting and pleasurable determine the content of what has to be learnt. After all the child might develop an aversion to science as many do!

Spencer's attempt to improve on Pestalozzi by spelling out the principles which govern intellectual development is presented as though it were a piece of psychology. But this is implausible. Most of them look like logical or conceptual points presented as empirical laws of development. Is it conceivable, for instance, that the complex should precede the simple in learning? How could anyone understand the concept of a triangle without understanding what a line is? Could anyone properly understand the abstract concept of a triangle without any familiarity with concrete examples of triangles? To have a full concept of 'triangle' requires being able to recognise instances of triangles as well as being able to relate it to other concepts. Indeed an important criterion of whether anyone has a full concept of a triangle is whether he can recognise instances. Could this happen without concrete instances being presented? Similarly, empirical generalisations must precede the rational stage of a science because they provide the material to be unified by theoretical principles. And so on. Nevertheless, whatever their status, teachers of Spencer's time often neglected these important principles, versions of which can be found in Plato's analogies of the Line and Cave, and which have been a commonplace since the work of Piaget.

Spencer, like Rousseau, stressed the importance of the self-development of the child, noting the number of things that children learn 'by discovery' without being told. Frequent telling, he argued, generates a disgust for knowledge and the general helplessness of the child. In his advocacy of 'discovery' Spencer seemed to have in mind the haphazard picking-up of things by children as well as the more disciplined self-development of a self-made man like himself. This type of 'discovery' on the part of children contrasts markedly with modern 'discovery methods' in which a child is brought to understand a principle in mathematics and science in a highly structured situation. This is a form of teaching which does not employ telling, but which brings the child to understand what is considered to be of importance. Spencer's type of 'discovery' might well be of many things that might do nothing to forward his development. His attack on telling, like Rousseau's, was an over-reaction against the formal teaching methods of the day. But to ban it altogether seems both unnecessary and doctrinaire. Children's incessant questions at certain ages indicate that they want to be told things. Telling, like any other teaching method – for instance, 'discovery methods' – should be employed judiciously, depending on the child and on the subject-matter. The greatest mistake about teaching methods is to suppose that there is just one desirable method of bringing about learning.

(4) MORAL EDUCATION

Spencer started his essay on moral education with a few generalities to set the scene. He denied, for instance, the contention that children are born good, believing the opposite to be nearer the mark; for children have evil impulses even if they are innocent with regard to knowledge. Heredity also plays a large part in moral character and the difficulties of moral education are the result of the combined faults of children and parents. There is also the influence of the world at a particular time. Too much rectitude would make life intolerable in the world as it is now. Reforms in domestic government must proceed, *pari passu*, with other reforms.

The main reform which Spencer wanted to see in domestic government was the substitution of learning from 'natural consequences' for learning from authoritative directions. A child running against a table or burning his hand in the fire is provided by Nature as a paradigm of moral discipline. There are the injurious effects which, on Spencer's utilitarian theory, make it bad and the causal connection which reveals Nature at work. The painful reaction is proportionate to the transgression and there are no threats – just a silent, rigorous performance. In a similar way an unskilful youth loses his job, unpunctuality has undesirable repercussions and an inattentive doctor finds himself with diminishing patients. 'Bitter experiences' are the most efficient penalties and contrast favourably with the artificial punishments of the penal system.

In these examples, Spencer argued, we have the guiding principles of moral education. Parents are to be ministers and interpreters of Nature. They must see that children habitually experience the true consequences of their actions. A bit of anger and scolding may go on as well, as it is a natural parental reaction. But it should not take the place of 'natural reactions' proper. Examples would be to get the child to clear up the litter he had made instead of just grumbling at him, leaving a child behind who is not ready for a walk, doing without things that are broken or lost. The child, in such cases, will feel that the evil is of his own making. Through a proper appreciation of cause and effect the impersonal agency of Nature is substituted for the personal agency of parents.

With graver offences such as theft and lying a degree of love-withdrawal on the part of the parent, who has a good relationship with the child, may be appropriate. But there is also the direct consequence of making restitution for the theft. The employment of the method of 'natural consequences' must be judicious. The aim of discipline is to produce a self-governing being. But no parent can let a 3-year-old boy play with an open razor. In infancy a fair degree of absolutism is necessary. This must diminish as intelligence grows. Thus, as in the history of political rule, there is a slow transition from external to internal discipline.

What is to be made of these proposals, which are a more systematic development of Rousseau's proposals on the same subject, exemplified in his suggestion that if Emile breaks his bedroom windows he should be allowed to suffer the consequent cold? The underlying doctrine in ethics, that it is only the consequences of actions in terms of harm or benefit that make them right or wrong, must be left on one side. Space does not permit a critique of utilitarianism and the doctrine presents problems enough without raising such fundamental issues. To start with: what is a 'natural consequence'? It is easy to see this in the case of burning the hand in the fire; for Nature is obviously involved as well as a crude causal generalisation. But what is the similarity between this and tidying up litter if a child makes a mess? For (1) tidiness is a requirement that human beings impose; it is not a feature of the natural world like fire; (2) an equally 'natural consequence', speaking analogously, would be for the child to have to wallow in and trip up over his own litter as to tidy it up. There is no semblance of a causal law that would dictate one reaction rather than another. What he would be required to do would depend upon what his parents thought appropriate.

Punctuality is another norm or human requirement that is observed more or less strictly in different countries and by different individuals. Trains are meant to go strictly on time, but the individual who arrives late may find that the train is late also. In some districts, too, a train or bus driver will wait for a tardy passenger whom he sees hurrying to catch it. Human life is constituted largely by an interlocking pattern of norms and conventions. Their operation, and how people react to them and to breaches of them, is not at all uniform and bears little resemblance to the 'silent rigorous performance' of the natural order.

The notion of 'natural consequences' modelled on the causal laws of the natural order has not, therefore, strict application to the social order. It is a further example of Spencer's tendency to treat human beings as organisms rather than as social animals. Another case which shows the variability of reactions within the social order is Spencer's case of theft. Some might think that restitution on the part of the child might be an appropriate consequence; others might argue that if the child had one of his possessions taken from him this would be a more appropriate 'natural consequence'. But to say that the parent or teacher was a 'minister of Nature' in either case would be more or less meaningless.

Spencer argued that 'natural consequences' are always just. But this is not necessarily so. Emile might catch pneumonia instead of just having a cold night as a consequence of his broken window. There is also the question of motive which created notorious difficulties for utilitarians. If an older child takes a toy from a younger child because it contains lead and the younger child is sucking it, his action might be treated as one of theft, with all the 'natural consequences' appropriate to it. But a closer consideration of the action, which took account of its motive, would reveal the inappropriateness of looking at it in this way. The careful inspection of motives would introduce all sorts of difficulties for the doctrine of 'natural consequences'. For what causal laws connect the two? Also superficially similar actions, done from different motives, might, on occasions have similar consequences.

The plausibility of Spencer's doctrine derived from two sources. First, there is the intuitive notion that the punishment should fit the offence. Hence the appropriateness of the child tidying up his own litter or making restitution in the case of theft. These are not 'natural consequences' but the demands of the moral consciousness – at least of some people's. Secondly, and more important, if the various rules and customs which permeate the social world are ignored or broken, conformity is more likely to be brought about by letting the child experience consequences – mainly social ones – than by lecturing and authoritative pronouncements. If a child is not punctual for an outing and is left behind he will probably learn more from such an experience than from a lecture on the importance of punctuality. But, as has been explained, these are not natural consequences as evident in the natural world. They are consequences dependent upon the very varied reactions of human beings to breaches of rules and conventions. There is, too, the danger that too much reliance on them would develop cleverness at anticipating and avoiding consequences rather than a deepening of the moral consciousness.

There are three very important aspects of moral education that Spencer omitted in his concentration on 'natural consequences'. First, he says nothing of the importance of approval when children do what is right. This is a very important source of positive encouragement and does much to build up the child's self-respect which is a crucial element in his conception of a self-governing individual. Secondly, he says nothing about the crucial role of imitation and modelling, by means of which so much is picked up from parents, teachers and older children. In both omissions there is further evidence of Spencer's atomic individualism. The child on his own learns best from 'natural consequences' of which parents and teachers are ministers. The notion of being initiated into a social life which they personify is alien to Spencer's way of thinking. Thirdly, he says nothing of the role of giving reasons with older children. There is nothing between despotism and natural consequences. Stock appeals like 'How would you like it if your brother stole your toy?' or pointing out the suffering to others that a course of action may entail do not feature.

CONCLUSION

This essay has been an attempt to ascertain whether Herbert Spencer's *Essays on Education* contain anything of permanent as distinct from contemporary significance. Certainly his essay on *'Physical education'*, which deals with diet, exercise and so on, and which I have omitted, did not. But what about the other three essays?

In the main there was little new in the essays on 'Intellectual education' and 'Moral education'. They were elegant and well-ordered restatements of the doctrines of Rousseau, Pestalozzi, and other progressive educators. What was distinctive of them was the attempt to fit these doctrines into an evolutionary framework and to relate them to the overall end of 'complete living'. His essay on 'Intellectual education', in which he tried to state Pestalozzi's insights in a more orderly fashion, confused psychological with logical issues, and his essay on 'Moral education', in which he tried to state Rousseau's doctrine of 'natural consequences' coherently, failed to distinguish the different ways in which the natural and social orders operate.

His best-known essay on 'What knowledge is of most worth?' is of more permanent importance, not for the answer which he gave to his own question but for the considerations which he raised in answering it. At the present time when schools and universities are being lambasted by politicians and industrialists about the shortage of scientifically educated manpower, Spencer's vigorous plea for more science and mathematics on the curriculum seems most pertinent. But it is one thing to agree with Spencer about the great importance of science to the individual and to the nation; it is quite another to argue that it has most worth as a form of knowledge. It has been suggested that the question is really unanswerable because it involves an abstraction from a complicated social activity. Science is not a matter of 'individual reason'; it is a social activity inseparable from moral principles of procedure and from the understanding of other people. Morality also determines the ends for which science is used. So science cannot be considered in isolation from the other forms of knowledge – morality and understanding other people – without which it could not proceed. There is then the problem of the criterion of 'worth'. Even if some form of utilitarianism, such as Spencer's, is adopted, in which morality becomes the adjustment of acts to ends, ends which science might help to bring about, the ends or end themselves cannot be established scientifically as Sidgwick, the most discerning of the utilitarians, saw when he argued that utilitarianism must rest on axioms derived from philosophical intuitionism. Spencer held an evolutionary view and believed fervently that evolution was moving towards the end of individual happiness or 'complete living'.

Nevertheless, though Spencer confused ethics with evolution, postulating such an end did give him a criterion by reference to which he could determine what should be on the curriculum. We can leave aside the difficult question about happiness as the end of life and education and ask the question what sorts of knowledge will a person predictably require *qua* person in dealing with the common contingencies of life. Spencer's list, apart from his treatment of aesthetic subjects just as leisure-time pursuits, is not a bad start. The individual will need to know how his body works, about health and disease; a knowledge of child-rearing will be important; he or she should have some broad-based vocational preparation; he should be prepared for citizenship and become cognisant of the workings of society. Spencer's great omission, apart from morality, was knowledge of other people. He was also a bit parochial, like Dewey, in including only studies of immediate concern and saying little of subjects such as geography and astronomy which locate human life in a wider context. Education should have application to a person's life but it should also concern itself with the wider context in which this life has to be lived. Literature and poetry, which Spencer regarded just as adornments, have also much to contribute in opening up vistas of this wider context.

So though one may disagree with Spencer's answer to his own question he did at least introduce considerations which are extremely relevant today with the proliferation of subjects on the curriculum. If one takes a modern attempt to tidy up such subjects by introducing the notion of 'forms of knowledge'[11] Spencer's question still stands. For which of the seven or eight 'forms of knowledge' are to be emphasised? What content is to be selected from science, history, mathematics, and so on? Relevance to 'complete living' may not provide a satisfactory answer; but at least, in Spencer's interpretation, it was more determinate in what it dictated in the way of content than Hirst's 'development of the rational mind'. For that could be done by taking almost any content from within the various forms. Spencer saw rightly that the content of education must be related to predictable features of the human condition. This was the importance of his essay rather than his ingenious arguments to show that all knowledge was a form of science. The details of his proposals were warped by his scientism, evolutionary faith, and by his atomic individualism. But his major conviction about the concern of education is of permanent significance.

REFERENCES: CHAPTER 4

1 See Kazamias, A., *Herbert Spencer on Education* (Columbia, New York: Teachers College Press, 1966), pp. 49–63.
2 Spencer, H., *Essays on Education* (London: Everyman edn, Dent, 1911) p. 93.
3 Sidgwick, H., *Lectures on the Ethics of T. H. Green, Mr. Herbert Spencer and J. Martineau* (London: Macmillan, 1902).
4 See pp. 35–6
5 Spencer, op. cit., p. 6.
6 ibid., p. 20.
7 ibid., p. 25.
8 James, W., *Psychology: A Briefer Course* (New York: Henry Holt, 1892), p. 468.
9 See Peters, R.S. (ed), *Brett's History of Psychology* (London: Allen & Unwin, 1962), pp. 660–6.
10 Spencer, op. cit., p. 41.
11 See Hirst, P.H., *Knowledge and the Curriculum* (London: Routledge & Kegan Paul, 1974).

Chapter 5

John Dewey's Philosophy of Education*

INTRODUCTION

It would be tempting to regard John Dewey's philosophy of education as an extrapolation of key features of learning situations in the old rural life, in which he was nurtured, to schooling in the industrial society which developed during his lifetime. Dewey experienced the new schooling at first hand as a not very successful teacher and was appalled by the rote learning, regimentation and irrelevance to life that characterised so much that went on. His philosophy, it might be said, was an attempt to introduce into this new institution the problem-solving, do-it-yourself method of the learning of his boyhood, together with the close link between learning and living and the sense of contributing to a social whole permeated by shared experiences.

No doubt there is some truth in this suggestion; for people's views about an educational situation are very much influenced by early models which they encounter. Michael Oakeshott, for instance, confessed at the end of an article on 'Learning and teaching'[1] that he owed his recognition of the values of patience, accuracy, economy, elegance and style to a sergeant gymnastics instructor, 'not on account of anything he said', but because he exemplified them.

The key to understanding Dewey's philosophy of education, however, is not just his early experience nor the obvious point that he was a pragmatist who applied the doctrines of Charles Peirce and William James in a straightforward way to education. Rather it is the realisation that he was, for a long time, a Hegelian who *later* became converted to pragmatism. Dewey, like Hegel, could not tolerate dualisms. He had a passion for unifying doctrines that, on the surface, seemed irreconcilable. Pragmatism, and especially its emphasis on scientific method, together with categories of thought extrapolated from biology, seemed to him the key to unification. It is also seemed a natural extension of his early experiences of problem-solving.

In his educational theory this passion for unification, for getting rid

*My thanks are due to my colleagues Pat White and Robert Dearden for their helpful comments on a first revision of this essay.

of dualisms, had ample scope as the titles of his books indicate: *The Child and the Curriculum*², *The School and Society*,³ *Interest and Effort in Education*,⁴ *Experience and Education*,⁵ and so on. This quest for unity, which Dewey substituted for the despised quest for certainty, explains why Dewey was not a wholehearted supporter of the progressive movement in America and ended up by writing his *Experience and Education*, which was highly critical of some of its practices.

(1) INDIVIDUAL GROWTH AND SHARED EXPERIENCES

The exception might seem to be *Democracy and Education*,⁶ which is a puzzling book, for there is plenty about education in it but very little about democracy – no proper discussion of liberty, equality and the rule of law, no probing of the problems of representation, participation and the control of the executive. The explanation of this is that Dewey viewed democracy mainly as a way of life; he was not particularly interested in the institutional arrangements necessary to support it. This way of life, he claimed, had two main features. First, it was characterised by numerous and varied shared interests and concerns. These play an important role in social control. Second, there is full and free interaction between social groups, with plenty of scope for communication.⁷ This is surely a strange characterisation of democracy. What is significant about it, however, is the emphasis on the social. Dewey later says:

> And the idea of perfecting an 'inner' personality is a sure sign of social divisions. What is called inner is simply that which does not connect with others – which is not capable of free and full communication. What is termed spiritual culture has usually been futile, with something rotten about it, just because it has been conceived as a thing which a man might have internally – and therefore exclusively. What one is as a person is what one is as associated with others, in a free give and take of intercourse.⁸

There is nothing particularly surprising about this in view of Dewey's background in idealism. Indeed it is very reminiscent of Bradley's attack on individualism in his famous chapter on 'My station and its duties'.⁹ Also the distinction between the public and the private has never been so sharply drawn in American society as in Europe. A modern symptom of this is that in a typical American township they have no walls to their gardens. But the puzzle is to reconcile this emphasis on 'shared experiences' and social approval and disapproval, as one of the main moulders of character, which Dewey emphasises, with his view of education as individual growth.

Much has been written about the unsatisfactoriness of this biological metaphor which Dewey used to impose unity of his theorizing. He argued that growth does not have an end but *is* an end. Thus education is not necessarily a matter of age; for education means the enterprise of supplying the conditions which ensure growth, or adequacy of life, irrespective of age. Living has its own intrinsic quality, whether in youth or in maturity, and the business of education is with that quality.

But, it is usually objected, how can 'growth' provide *criteria* of this quality? Did not Napoleon or the Marquis de Sade 'grow'? Dewey faced this problem in *Experience and Education*[10] and argued that growth in efficiency as a burglar, as a gangster, or as a corrupt politician does not lead to further growth. Growth in general is retarded by such limited forms of growth. This answer did not help him much as many have pointed out, with imaginative sketches of the developing life-styles of burglars, train robbers, and so on. What he needed was other criteria by reference to which desirable and undesirable forms of growth could be distinguished.

In fact I think that Dewey *did* have other criteria of value for education. His metaphor of 'growth', like his other concepts of 'interaction' and 'continuity', are just part of his conceptual apparatus, taken from biology, which symbolise his insistence that man is part of the natural world. He could not tolerate the dualism, found in thinkers such as Kant and Descartes, between man and nature, any more than he could tolerate other dualisms. But later in *Democracy and Education*[11] he reached what he called a 'technical definition' of 'education' as 'that reconstruction or reorganisation of experiences which adds to the meaning of experience, and which increases ability to direct the course of subsequent experience'. He went on to say that an activity which brings education or instruction with it makes one aware of some of the *connections* which had been imperceptible. He stressed the addition in *knowledge* both of the child who reaches for a bright light and gets burned and of the scientist learning more about fire in his laboratory. In brief Dewey's main concern was with growth in practical *knowledge*, in the development of critical intelligence as described in his earlier popular book *How We Think*.[12]

But Dewey, as a pragmatist, was also interested in what he called 'the other side of an educative experience' which is the 'added power of direction or control'. He contrasted this with aimless activity, on the one hand, and singled out acting under external direction as a classic example of this, and with routine activity on the other hand, which only increases skill in doing a particular thing. This could be interpreted as a way of stressing the virtue of autonomy, or self-initiated action which is the outcome of independent thought. Indeed, Dr. Dearden, in his *The Philosophy of Primary Education*,[13] sees autonomy as the ethical value which is embedded in the whole growth ideology. What is common to both is the notion of self-originated activity. This is certainly a valid interpretation of many other more individualistic theorists who made use of the metaphor of 'growth'. But I doubt whether it completely fits Dewey with his continued emphasis on 'shared experiences' and communication. I think his ideal was much more that of a group of dedicated, problem-solving scientists, who were united by their shared concerns and willingness to communicate their findings to each other. The 'lonely will' of the individual was anathema to him,[14] though in Chapter 5 of *Experience and Education* he does extol the virtue of 'freedom' understood as self-control, whilst pointing out that too much freedom understood negatively as the absence of social constraints may be destructive of shared co-operative activities. I think that he more or less took for granted the value of individual self-determination but was more concerned to stress the values of *co-operative* problem-solving as an antidote to the extremes of individualism in the old pioneer period.

This interpretation of Dewey's concept of education not only gives more determinateness to his somewhat nebulous metaphor of 'growth'; it also explains the link which he forged between education and his rather strange conception of the democratic way of life. His emphasis, in the latter, on numerous shared interests and communication makes sense if it is seen as a projection of features of the kinds of communities in which he worked and lived. For Dewey was an academic who, as well as writing forty books and about seven hundred articles, was constantly founding and joining groups concerned with various forms of social and educational reform. Thus growth for him was not growth in *any* direction which would be consistent with his claim that desirable growth is that which permits more growth; it is rather growth in practical critical thought, which opens up the possibility of more control of the environment. But this is not something which the individual does on his own. In his early days at Michigan one of Dewey's colleagues was G.H. Mead, whose theories about the social nature of the self and the social determinants of thought influenced Dewey profoundly. These theories strengthened Dewey's Hegelian convictions about the social nature of man and supplied support for his own distinctive brand of pragmatism, with its emphasis on 'shared experiences'. It enabled him to argue that growth, properly understood, can only flourish in a democratic environment. Indeed, to use a Platonic metaphor, for Dewey the democratic way of life is growth 'writ large'. There is unity discernible beneath the appearances of democracy and education.

(2) INDIVIDUAL INTEREST AND EXTERNAL DIRECTION

Dewey's attempt to transcend dualisms is nowhere more apparent than in his treatment of the teaching situation.

(a) Aims of education

There is first of all his treatment of aims of education in which he attacked the false dichotomy between means and ends which he exposed at greater length in his *Human Nature and Conduct*.[15] But he had additional concerns in his educational writings. First, he insisted on the intrinsic value of educational activities. They are not merely unavoidable means to something else.[16] Second, he maintained that good aims arise from what is going on, from the purposes of the pupil. They must not be externally imposed, or ready-made. Nevertheless he did not advocate a kind of free for all in which *any* aims are accepted if they arise in this way. They must be capable of translation into a method of co-operating with those undergoing instruction; they must lend themselves to the construction of specific procedures. And who is to be the judge of this unless it is the teacher? Also Dewey realised that such aims do not spring spontaneously from the nature of the child. Indeed, he criticised Rousseau for making Nature his god. They are moulded by what he called 'the social medium'. Although he was critical of imitation as an important factor in 'the social medium' he admitted the large influence of social approval and disapproval.[17] Thus all along the line Dewey tried to combine the progressive child-centred approach with what he had learnt from Mead and with what was in his bones as a Hegelian. He resisted external *direction* and *imposition*, but insisted on the importance of external approval and encouragement. He thus achieved some kind of reconciliation between the progressive and traditional views of teaching.

(b) Teaching methods

This attempt to get rid of dualisms was made even more explicit in his *Experience and Education*[18] He was at pains to point out that he was not suggesting a passive or spectatorial role for the teacher. Indeed he argued that 'basing education upon personal experience may mean more multiplied and more intimate contacts between the mature and the immature than ever existed in the traditional school, and consequently more rather than less guidance by others'.[19] In their account of Dewey's laboratory school the authors insist that 'Those planning the activities must see each child as an ever changing person . . . They must carefully select and grade the materials used, altering such selection, as is necessary in all experimentation.'[20] (This was practicable because of the extremely favourable teacher–pupil ratio. The school started with three regular teachers for thirty–two children; rose to sixteen teachers for sixty children, and ended with twenty–three teachers plus ten assistants for a hundred and forty children!)

Dewey himself described this careful grading and selection of material in terms of his two criteria of educative experiences, 'interaction' and 'continuity'. He used the term 'interaction', rather than more homely terms such as 'needs' and 'purposes' of the child not purely because of his desire to create some kind of biological unity between the processes of education and those of life but also because too many progressives, in his opinion, had neglected the objective conditions of the situations and the role of the teacher in arranging for them to match the internal conditions of the child. Similarly continuity was stressed because it was not sufficient for the child to be interested in anything; interests had to be explored which were rich in possibilities for future experiences. So 'guidance' by the teacher was substituted for the 'external direction' of traditional methods. And because interests arose from the child, deriving from his 'impulses' of investigation and experimentation, constructiveness, expressiveness and the social impulse,[21] the approach could claim to be child-centred.

The method of learning which conformed to these criteria of 'educative experiences' was that of problem-solving, a detailed account of which was given by Dewey in *How We Think*. This stress on problem-solving as a method was later taken up by Kilpatrick and formalised in the project method. Dewey was favourably disposed towards it but did not become a passionate advocate of it. To be fair to him he was always very guarded about details of teaching methods. He confined himself to generalities, knowing that details of implementation must vary with individuals.

(c) Social control and the role of the teacher
Dewey's account of the social control of the teacher exhibited the same tendency towards unification. He tried to transcend the dichotomy between the 'keeping order' view of the traditional school and the self-imposed discipline advocated by the progessives. He compared children in a classroom to their participation in a game. Games involve rules and children do not feel that they are submitting to external imposition in obeying them. The control of the actions of the participating individuals is affected by the whole situation in which individuals are involved, in which they share and of which they are co-operative or interacting parts.

The teacher exercises authority in such a situation as the representative and agent of the interests of the group as a whole. If he or she has to take firm action it is done on behalf of the interests of the group, not as an exhibition of personal power. In the traditional school the teacher had to 'keep order' because order was in the teacher's keeping instead of residing in the shared work being done. In the new schools the main job of the teacher is to think and plan ahead so that knowledge of individuals may be married with knowledge of subject-matter that will enable activities to be selected which lend themselves to social organisation. Thus 'the teacher loses the position of external boss or dictator but takes on that of leader of group acitivities'.[22]

(3) THE CONTENT OF EDUCATION AND THE ROLE OF THE SCHOOL

Dewey is sometimes classified with those progressives who have extolled following the interests of the child at the expense of subject-matter. This is completely to misunderstand his position. For he was too much of a Hegelian to ignore the importance of a society's 'cultural heritage' which he described as 'the ripe fruitage of experiences'. But, again as a Hegelian, he strove to remove the dichotomy between both 'the child' and 'the curriculum' and 'the school' and 'society'. On the one hand, therefore, he insisted that the curriculum should embody what he called the sociological and the psychological principles. The sociological principle demanded that the pupil be initiated into the customs, habits, values and knowledge which constitute the culture of a community. The psychological principle demanded that this should be done with due regard to the pupil's individual needs, interests and problems.

On the other hand he believed passionately that the curriculum should be socially relevant. It should contribute to making children active members of a democratic society. Indeed on this theme Dewey waxed almost mystical and poetic: 'When the school introduces and trains each child of society into membership within such a little community, saturating him with the spirit of service, and providing him with the instruments of effective self-direction, we shall have the deepest and best guarantee of a larger society, which is worthy, lovely and harmonious.'[23] Let us, therefore, consider in more detail his resolution of the dichotomies between the child and the curriculum and between the school and society.

(*a*) *The child and the curriculum*
Most of what Dewey wrote about the curriculum related to the elementary school and much of it seems rather dated. But it illustrates well his approach. He stressed, first of all, the importance of practical activities such as sewing, cooking, weaving, carpentry and metalwork. These conformed to the sociological principle because they were basic to life, being concerned with food, clothing, and so on, and thus part of the cultural heritage. They also conformed to the psychological principle for two reasons. First, Dewey was convinced that children are interested in them. Second, they embody motor activities which Dewey considered to be closely connected with mental development as a whole. Also, from an educational point of view, they were capable of providing continuity in that they could open up all sorts of other fruitful studies. As he put it: 'You can concentrate the history of all mankind into the evolution of the flax, cotton and wool fibres into clothing.'[24]

In addition to practical activities he included some traditional 'subjects' in the curriculum with the proviso that they should be related to his concept of man as a problem-solving animal concerned with control over his environment. Thus he regarded geography as being of particular importance – but as a way of gaining in power to perceive the spatial, the natural connections of an ordinary act. History was acceptable, too, as a way of recognising the human connections of ordinary acts.[25] And both, of course, must start from the child's immediate interests – geography must move outwards from local geography and history from 'some present situation with its problems.'[26]

Science is, of course, included, but subject to the same sort of provisos. It should be taught with the psychological principle in mind and start from the everyday experience of the learner. There was too much of a tendency to teach it in the logical order of the developed study. Above all science should be taught as the agency of progress in action. For it opens up new ends as well as helping mankind to achieve existing ones. Because of science man can now 'face the future with a firm belief that intelligence properly used can do away with evils once thought inevitable'.[27]

Finally the curriculum should include communication skills such as reading, writing, mathematics and foreign languages. These appealed to the child's 'impulses' to express himself and to share his experiences with others. So the best time to teach him the techniques of communication is when the need to communicate is vitally important to him. These communication skills should be taught incidentally as the need arose.

(b) *The School and Society*

There were two aspects of Dewey's attempt to resolve the dualism between the school and society. The first dealt with the relationship of the school to the home and surrounding community, the second with its relationship to the wider society which the pupil would enter on leaving school. On the first aspect, as I said at the beginning, Dewey was greatly impressed by the informal type of learning that went on in the home and in the small rural communities that were passing. He frequently contrasted this natural way of learning, in which there was no separation between learning and life, with the artificial drills and recitations of formal schooling. His plea was that there should be an indissoluble link between learning in school and learning out of school.[28] Dewey's insistence that the school itself should be a real community, exhibiting numerous shared interests and open communication, was his answer to the other question of the school's relationship to the wider society. The school itself should be a miniature democracy, according to his understanding of 'democracy'. He saw this type of school not only as valuable in itself, because of the quality of life that it made possible, but also as the springboard to social progress.

Dewey took a prominent part in the current controversy about trade schools and vocational education.[29] He deprecated, of course, the split between the practical and the liberal which reflected an undesirable type of class-structure. He objected to the implicit suggestion that education should be made subservient to the demands of interested manufacturers. Nevertheless, his solution was typically one in which the dualism between vocational and liberal education could be resolved; for he argued that if more practical activities were introduced into schools, education would be through occupations and not for occupations. He advocated the introduction of processes involved in industrial life to make school life more active, more impregnated with science, and more in touch with the world. This should be part of everybody's education, not just a special provision for those who were singled out to become the modern equivalents of hewers of wood and drawers of water. Above all a different attitude to work should be developed so that young people would become imbued with a sense of community service instead of working only for private gain. It should 'train power of readaptation to changing conditions so that future workers would not become blindly subject to a fate imposed upon them'.[30]

(4) GENERAL COMMENTS

What is to be made of this intellectual edifice? For opinions about it are very varied. I once tried to get an eminent American philosopher interested in the philosophy of education. He grunted and remarked that John Dewey had set that subject up – and killed it stone dead! On the other hand Sidney Hook, another eminent American philosopher, published a book as recently as 1973 in which he included several essays in defence of Dewey.[31] He saw Dewey's philosophy as providing a middle road between radicals such as Reimer, Goodman and Illich and the post-sputnik traditionalists such as Vice-Admiral Rickover.

I agree with Sidney Hook that such a middle road is necessary, but I do not find the one sign posted by Dewey particularly convincing or congenial. For his way of resolving various dualisms by his account of the 'growth' of the problem-solving man has the character of a panacea which involves both distortion in the sphere of what he called the sociological principle and a romantic idealisation in the sphere of the psychological principle. The dualisms are not in fact resolved. Let me explain these criticisms before addressing myself to an estimate of his unifying ideal.

(a) The sociological principle

Dewey admitted the importance of making the child aware of his cultural heritage but only on the condition that he should be introduced to it in a way which stressed its relevance to present practical and social problems. This is understandable as said against unimaginative rote learning of classical textbooks, but, if taken seriously, is a good recipe for failing to understand what we have inherited. For it fails to take account of the degree of autonomy which some traditions of inquiry have from contemporary practical problems. Understanding depends upon entering imaginatively into the mind of those who have contributed to these traditions and grasping what their problems were as arising from them. Copernicus and Kepler, for instance, were both working within the Pythagorean tradition. The heliocentric theory emerged because it was mathematically simpler; Kepler's second law of planetary motion was lighted on in the course of speculations about the music of the heavenly bodies. To stress the relevance of these momentous advances for navigation or space travel does nothing towards understanding them as theories. It may be said that the point is not so much to understand such theories thoroughly, but to use them. But a failure to understand properly the problems with which people in the past have been concerned often leads to absurdities in attempts to use them.

Piaget, for instance, was greatly influenced by Kant. Piaget's theories are widely applied in the educational sphere in a ham-handed way because the educationalist in question has no conception of what Kant was about in his critiques. The school, surely, should not concern itself only with what is relevant to contemporary problems. It should *also* distance itself a bit from these and introduce children to speculations about the world in science, and to insights into the human condition in literature and history, which are of perennial significance. The dualism is there and gives rise to continuing tensions.

Dewey's view of the teacher, who is society's agent for the transmission and development of its cultural heritage, is also unsatisfactory. For it slurs over the dualism between the teacher's position as an authority and the legitimate demand for 'participation'. A teacher is not just a leader in a game like a football captain. In a game most of the participants know how to play; but pupils come to a teacher because they are ignorant, and he or she is meant to be, to some extent, an authority on some aspect of the culture. This disparity between teacher and taught – especially in the primary school – makes talk of 'democracy in education' problematic, unless 'democracy' is watered down to mean just multiplying shared experiences and openness of communication, as by Dewey. If 'democracy' is to include, as it usually does, some suggestion of participation in decision-making, we are then confronted with current tensions underlying the question of how much 'participation' is compatible with the freedom and authority of the teacher.

Dewey himself never paid much attention to institutional issues. This was not just because he lived before the days when 'participation' became an issue. It was also because his attitude towards the democratic way of life was semi-mystical. 'When the emotional force, the mystic force, one might say, of the miracles of the shared life and shared experience is spontaneously felt, the hardness and concreteness of contemporary life will be bathed in a light that never was on land or sea.'[32] I wonder if he felt like this about sitting on committees!

(b) The psychological principle

Dewey's treatment of the psychological principle was equally unsatisfactory; for it combined a conception of the child, which was almost as idealistic as his conception of democracy, with a too-limited view of what he called 'the social medium'. This led him to oversimplify the dualism between what he called 'internal conditions' and what is the result of social influences. Dewey was impressed, as I have reiterated, by the informal learning that went on in the home and in the local community and wanted to forge a link between this sort of learning and learning at school. But he did not ask the questions 'which home?' and 'which local community?'. For sociologists have catalogued the vast disparities that exist between homes in this respect.

Dewey's account of the ideal educational situation assumed, to start with, an 'impulse' to investigate and experiment, as well as a 'social impulse' from which co-operation stems. Maybe most of the children in his laboratory school had such impulses. Maybe all children have them at birth. But by the time they get to school it is noticeable how many children seem to lack these 'impulses'. And this is probably due to the *absence* of eager learning at home. Secondly, as Dewey pointed out, there may not be much potentiality for 'growth' in some problem which actually bothers a child. So the teacher must try to divert him on to some other problem. Teachers come to know from experience, on the grapevine, or from books which topics present rich possibilities for a project. So those going round schools find that, miraculously, children in many different schools seem to be bothered about water, costume, or flight! So in fact projects can become just as standardised and externally imposed as straightforward instruction.

This, on a broader view than Dewey's, is not a damaging objection to the use of projects and the problem-solving method generally; for one of the gifts of the teacher is to stimulate interest and to get pupils to regard as problematic situations which they never previously viewed in this light. What Dewey called 'interaction' is not just a function of *existing* 'internal conditions' within the pupil. There is the problem, too, that if existing 'internal conditions' are taken as seriously as the desirability of co-operation, a highly individualised curriculum would be the result which would require something like the very favourable teacher–pupil ratio of the Dewey school and which might also mean that many pupils ended up with vast gaps in their knowledge. The same idealistic outlook is evident in Dewey's treatment of the problem of social control, which, for many teachers nowadays, is a constant source of strain. When talking of the problem of unruly children Dewey remarks that 'There are likely to be some who, when they come to school, are already victims of injurious conditions outside of the school.'[33] But this does not apply just to odd individuals; it applies to a vast multitude of children who come to school with an attitude towards learning which makes it very difficult for the teacher to contrive a situation in the classroom that approximates to a game in which they eagerly participate. Similarly the one thing which they expect of the teacher is that he or she will be able to 'keep order'. The attitude towards authority, which is determined by the control system of their homes, makes it very difficult for them to take seriously a teacher who regards himself or herself just as a friendly guide to ensure continuity in their shared experiences of problem-solving. It takes a very skilful teacher to resocialise such children so that they are ready to learn in the way of which Dewey approved. I mention this rather mundane criticism because I do not think that he conceived of himself as putting forward an ideal which could only be realised in a school like his own laboratory school, which catered for children whose home backgrounds were rich in experience and favourable towards learning. His message was that the school could transform society; so I think he thought that this type of learning situation could be generalised straightaway. It is at this point that my scepticism grows.

Another defect in Dewey's treatment of the 'social medium' and of his slurring over the dualism between the child's 'internal conditions' and what he gets from others is his dismissal of imitation as being of much importance.[34] If this is extended to include identification it can work both negatively and positively for the teacher. The negative aspect is that so many of the models in society, with whom children identify, are anti-educational from Dewey's point of view. He always argued that education provides its own ends; is not merely a means to money, prestige, or a good job. Yet the child is constantly presented with models of people who have got on in the world. The questions 'What is the payoff?' or 'Where does this get you?' are asked about almost anything. It is very tempting, therefore, for the teacher to make use of extrinsic motivations such as marks, prizes, competition, and so on, perhaps refined by Skinnerian techniques, in order to get children to learn. For, because of the ethos of individualistic societies, and the models which they throw up, these forms of motivation are readily understood. Co-operating with others in shared experiences because of their intrinsic value has not, unfortunately, the same straightforward appeal.

On the positive side, however, imitation and identification can work for the teacher if he or she has mastery of and enthusiasm for what is being taught. A good example of this is the case of Oakeshott and the sergeant gymnastics instructor which I mentioned at the start. Dewey, I suspect, was hostile to imitation because it smacks of external imposition. But it is rather cavalier for a thinker with an evolutionary orientation like Dewey to disregard one of the main mechanisms which the human race has evolved for the transmission of culture. Bronfenbrenner, for instance, in his *Two Worlds of Childhood*,[35] contrasts the USA and USSR from the point of view of the degree to which systematic modelling is encouraged. His chapter on 'The unmaking of the American child' makes very sobering reading.

Dewey was well aware of the features of industrial society that were inimical to his whole conception of democracy and of education. In his *Individualism Old and New*[36] he pointed out the irrelevance of the old individualistic values that had characterised the pioneer; for the present problem was not that of wrestling with physical nature but that of dealing with social conditions. Earlier individualism had shrunk to industrial initiative and ability in making money. This was the main enemy. What was needed was a *new* individualism. Dewey refrained from sketching what it would be like but suggested that technology, taken in its broadest sense, offers the main clue to its nature. For it would help both to transform society and to develop a new type of individual mind.

(c) The technological man
What, then, is to be our verdict on Dewey's ideal of the technological, problem-solving man which is central to understanding his convictions about the methods and content of education and his conception of democracy? Surely what was said of Bernard Shaw: 'He is like the *Venus de Milo*. What there is of him is admirable.'

There are two respects in which Dewey's ideal speaks very much to our condition. First, the plea for the use of practical intelligence, backed up by the use of science, to tackle social and economic problems, is as pertinent today as it was at the time at which he was writing. Second, his emphasis on 'shared experiences' and communication and his attack on the relics of the old individualism are apposite in a society dominated by frustration of the desire for material gain. We could do with more fraternity, the forgotten ideal of the French Revolution. But he was mistaken in thinking that the ideals of individualism have shrunk just to the desire for profit. There are also autonomy, integrity and authenticity which are still potent ideals both in life and in education. His playing-down of such ideals is surprising; for they can scarcely be dismissed as facets of the 'rottenness' of perfecting an inner personality. He says of aims of education that we do not emphasise things which do not require emphasis. He may well have thought this about such individualistic ideals.

(*i*) *Neglect of the personal and of the education of the emotions.* What, then, are the *defects* of this ideal? Mainly that, rather ironically, in putting forward an ideal which is meant to resolve current dualisms, he develops a very one-sided view of man that completely ignores certain features of the human condition. First, Dewey ignores the purely personal life of human beings. By that I do not mean just his failure to emphasise the importance of respect for persons in his account of democracy, nor his attack on the 'rottenness' of individual attempts at self-improvement; I mean also his neglect of interpersonal relationships and the education of the emotions. It is significant that he makes practically no mention of the role of literature in education. Literature is singularly unamenable to the problem-solving method of learning, and often concerns itself with the predicaments of man rather than with his problems. I once attended a poetry lesson in an American school. The teacher read part of Gray's *Elegy* beautifully and then opened up a somewhat desultory discussion on what a curfew was, and so on. I asked her why she did not read it again as she had such a lovely voice and had the pupils spell bound. 'Oh', she said, 'we are only allowed to read it once. It is meant to provide material for discussion and problem-solving to help the children to become democratic citizens.'

(*ii*) *Predicaments as well as problems.* This brings me to the second comment on Dewey's ideal – the emphasis on problem-solving. He shared the view of most Americans of that period that life presented mainly problems that could be solved, given the time and the technology. This optimism is of course waning somewhat, in the face of the intractability of problems connected with race, unemployment and poverty. But even if it were not, the view of life presented is one-sided, not to say exhausting. Dewey, of course, appreciated the importance of habit in life, but accorded no value to anything that was a matter of routine. Yet there is nothing particularly wicked about the conservative pleasures derived from repetition and familiarity. There are also the more distanced, aesthetic enjoyments that have little to do with problem-solving. There are many aspects of life, too, that present not problems that can be solved but predicaments that have to be lived with. If a man in his prime is afflicted by a coronary or loses his wife, he does not just have a problem.

(*iii*) *Disregard of the irrational.* The third criticism is like the second in that it is directed against Dewey's confident, reformist optimism. He completely ignores the fundamental irrationality of man. He never mentions Freud, who was a contemporary of his, and seems sublimely unaware of the diagnosis of the human condition that derived from his insights. The view that civilisation is a brittle crust containing with difficulty irrational yearnings made no impact on Dewey in spite of his active interest in the rise of nazism as a threat to democracy.[37]

(*iv*) *Defects of the pragmatic stance*. There are finally the defects of Dewey's pragmatic stance. Others have commented in detail on the defects of the pragmatic theory of truth.[38] I shall confine myself to more general issues, which are crucial to his educational ideal. Basically the pragmatist lacks reverence, is guilty of what Russell calls 'cosmic impiety'.[39] He sees Nature just as something that can be used for human purposes. He lacks a sense of awe and of wonder. This is manifest, too, in Dewey's insistence that history and geography must be taught subject to the condition that they throw light on contemporary problems and concerns. There is no reason why these should not be used as a starting point if they are motivationally potent, but to view such studies *only* under this aspect is both to distort them and to encourage a kind of present-centred hubris.

It is the same with science. Dewey actually grossly exaggerated the connection between scientific theories and everyday practical problems. But to represent scientific theories, which are some of the greatest products of the human imagination, just as aids to action, is to ignore a whole dimension of human life. His psychology is made to fit this emphasis; for the child is credited with an 'impulse' to investigate and experiment but not with a more generalised 'drive to know' with which modern psychologists credit even monkeys. So Dewey put into the child at the beginning in the form of 'impulses' what he took out at the end in the form of the co-operative communicative technological man. The dimensions of speculative curiosity, of wonder and awe, are missing.

I am not of course suggesting that technology is unimportant in comparison with disinterested speculation. Still less am I suggesting that 'relevance' is an unimportant criterion of learning and of the curriculum. What I am suggesting is that Dewey's ideal is as myopic as his conception of 'relevance'. Contributing to practical purposes is only *one* criterion of 'relevance'. The others are not limited to that which arouses plain curiosity; there are also countless studies in literature, religion, history, psychology and the social sciences which are of great emotional significance to human beings without being obviously connected with practical purposes. When Whitehead said that education is the 'acquisition of the art of the utilisation of knowledge'[40] I am sure that he did not think of 'utilisation' purely in terms of relevance to practical purposes. What he meant was that the content of education should have application to people's lives. It should not consist in 'inert ideas' propounded by teachers on the assumption that their pupils are going to be devotees of their subject like themselves. For one of the crucial questions for any teacher is what there is in his subject for the majority who are unlikely to become specialists in it.

CONCLUSION

To sum up: Dewey's revolt against the formalism and irrelevance of much that went on in schools is still pertinent. So is his plea for more 'shared experiences' and more development of practical intelligence. But his ideal of the technological man is too limited and culture-bound. It ignores whole dimensions of the human condition – especially the predicaments of man, his irrationality, and his emotional sensitivities and susceptibilities. The cult of co-operative action is a welcome antidote to the lonely quest for salvation or for private profit. But human beings inhabit a personal as well as a public world; they are circumscribed by a Nature that has to be accepted as well as transformed, that should be an object of enjoyment, of wonder and of awe as well as material to be mastered for human purposes. A balance has to be struck between personal preoccupations and public policies, between servile humility and masterful hubris. These are dualisms that Dewey did *not* resolve.

REFERENCES: CHAPTER 5

1 Oakeshott, M., 'Learning and teaching', in Peters, R.S. (ed.), *The Concept of Education* (London: Routledge & Kegan Paul, 1967).
2 Dewey, J., *The Child and the Curriculum* (Chicago: University of Chicago Press, 1902).
3 Dewey, J., *The School and Society* (Chicago: University of Chicago Press. 1900; rev. edns 1915, 1943).
4 Dewey, J., *Interest and Effort in Education* (Boston, Mass.: Houghton Mifflin, 1913.
5 Dewey, J., *Experience and Education* (New York: Macmillan, 1938).
6 Dewey, J., *Democracy and Education* (New York: Macmillan, 1916).
7 ibid., ch. VII.
8 ibid., p. 143.
9 Bradley, F.H., *Ethical Studies* (London: Oxford University Press, 1876), ch. V.
10 Dewey, *Experience and Education*.
11 Dewey, *Democracy and Education*, pp. 89–90.
12 Dewey, J., *How We Think* (Boston, Mass.: D.C. Heath, 1910).
13 Dearden, R.F., *The Philosophy of Primary Education* (London: Routledge & Kegan Paul, 1968).
14 Murdoch, I., *The Sovereignty of Good* (London: Routledge & Kegan Paul, 1970).
15 Dewey, J., *Human Nature and Conduct* (New York: Holt, 1922).
16 Dewey, *Democracy and Education*, p. 127.
17 ibid., pp. 41–2.
18 Dewey, *Experience and Education*.
19 ibid., p. 21.
20 Mayhew, K.C., and Edwards, A.C., *The Dewey School* (New York: Atherton Press, 1966), p. 22.

21 ibid., pp. 46, 41.
22 Dewey, *Experience and Education*, p. 59.
23 Dewey, *The School and Society* (7th impression, 1963), p. 29.
24 ibid., p. 22.
25 Dewey, *Democracy and Education*, p. 246.
26 ibid., p. 251.
27 ibid., p. 263.
28 Dewey, *The School and Society* (1963), p. 91.
29 Dykhuizen, G., *The Life and Mind of John Dewey* (Carbondale, Ill.: Southern Illinois University Press, 1973), pp. 141–3.
30 Dewey, *Democracy and Education*, p. 372.
31 Hook, S., *Education and the Taming of Power* (New York: Open Court, 1973).
32 Dewey, J., *Reconstruction in Philosophy* (New York: Holt, 1920), p. 211.
33 Dewey, *Experience and Education*, p. 56.
34 Dewey, *Democracy and Education*, pp. 40–3.
35 Bronfenbrenner, U., *Two Worlds of Childhood* (London: Allen & Unwin, 1971).
36 Dewey, J., *Individualism, Old and New* (New York: Minton, Baker & Co., 1936).
37 See Dykhuisen, op. cit., pp. 290–1.
38 See, for instance, Scheffler, I., *Four Pragmatists* (London: Routledge & Kegan Paul, 1974).
39 Russell, B., *A History of Western Philosophy* (London: Allen & Unwin, 1946), p. 856.
40 Whitehead, A.N., *The Aims of Education* (London: Macmillan, 1921; repr. New York: Mentor Books, 1949), p. 16.

Chapter 6

Michael Oakeshott's Philosophy of Education

There will always remain something of a mystery about how a tradition of political behaviour in learned . . .

M. Oakeshott

INTRODUCTION

On reading much modern analytical philosophy one is often tempted to reflect that there is too much technique and too little judgement, to use one of Oakeshott's cardinal distinctions. Technical competence is shown in making distinctions, but what is often lacking is a 'nose' for the distinctions on which anything of philosophical importance depends. Oakeshott's 'style' of philosophy exemplifies the obverse combination of virtue and vice. He almost always has something to say which is interesting and important; but his impressionistic and rather literary approach to philosophical analysis often leaves what he has to say in a somewhat shadowy state. Few modern philosophers, of course, write with Oakeshott's literary skill; their articles read like work-notes rather than pieces prepared for others to read. But Oakeshott's literary virtuosity sometimes involves a systematic elusiveness when he touches upon situations covered by his key concepts.

This elusiveness applies particularly to his concept of 'tradition', on which I have had occasion to comment elsewhere.[1] It applies also to certain key concepts in his philosophy of education such as 'judgement' and 'imparting', with which I shall be concerned in this chapter. Nevertheless Oakeshott almost always raises fundamental philosophical issues in an exciting way, and stimulates others to further thought about them. This is particularly true of his philosophy of education with most of which I have great sympathy; indeed my own views have been much influenced by his writings, though he would be the last person to demand much in the way of acknowledgement.

OAKESHOTT'S GENERAL CONCEPTION OF EDUCATION

In talking about education Oakeshott always starts, as is fitting for a philosopher of the idealist school, for whom history is of cardinal importance, with the civilised heritage of a people, with Hegel's 'second nature' composed of 'a stock of emotions, beliefs, images, ideas, manners of thinking, languages, skills, practices and manners of activity'[2] out of which the 'things' which confront us in our environment are generated. Education consists in the initiation of a new generation into this civilised heritage. But Oakeshott never views this initiation as a process of moulding people or of transmitting this heritage in an undiscriminating or routinised way. He usually draws attention to the activity of the learner by using homely phrases which avoid the jargon of 'self-realisation' and 'the development of individual potentialities'. A typical way of putting it is as follows:

> Education I will take to be the process of learning, in circumstances of direction and restraint, how to recognise and make something of ourselves. Unavoidably, it is a two-fold process in which we enjoy an initiation into what for want of a better word I will call a 'civilisation', and in doing so discover our own talents and aptitudes in relation to that civilisation and begin to cultivate and to use them. Learning to make something of ourselves in no context in particular is an impossibility; and the context appears not only in what is learned but also in the conditions of direction and restraint that belong to any education.[3]

This civilised heritage, within which the individual has to learn to make something of himself, Oakeshott sometimes discusses in terms of a conversation. 'If, then, we recognise education as an initiation into a civilisation, we may regard it as beginning to learn our way about a material, emotional, moral and intellectual inheritance, and as a learning to recognise the varieties of human utterance and to participate in the conversation they compose.'[4] He uses this metaphor in order to stress three points: first of all, the fact that there are different 'voices' – for example, those of science, poetry, history, morals – and secondly, the necessity for communication between those who, without opportunities for cross-disciplinary conversation, are in danger of confining their discussions to one mode of thought. He thinks that the main function of a university, as distinct from a graduate school or a technical college, is to provide the occasions and the facilities for a sustained conversation of this sort. This is his way of stressing the importance of what educationalists refer to in their jargon as 'developing the whole man'. He thinks, thirdly, that the metaphor of a conversation is appropriate because the relations between the voices are not those of assertion and denial 'but the conversational relationships of acknowledgement and accommodation'. By this, presumably, he means things such as that in a discussion of, for instance, a moral problem, a scientific generalisation can never of itself constitute a refutation of a moral assertion but can be relevant to it in certain ways. Arguments, or discussions, on the other hand, are structured in terms of one mode of thought.

Each of these 'voices' or modes of experience has what Oakeshott calls (perhaps somewhat misleadingly) a distinctive 'language' and 'literature' of its own. The language is, for example, 'the manner of thinking of a scientist'; the 'literature' is, for example, 'a textbook of geology or what may be called the current state of our geological knowledge'.[5] This distinction enables him to demarcate, in a rough and ready way, school, vocational and university education.

TYPES OF EDUCATION

School Education
School education is concerned, in Oakeshott's view, mainly with initiation into the different literatures. After acquiring basic skills the child begins to enjoy and even to use the intellectual capital of a civilisation. Much, however, is acquired that the child does not really know how to use. It is a capital which generates something valuable on its own account. 'Learning here is borrowing raw material the possible uses of which remain concealed.'[6] Oakeshott assigns a very specific function to school education which would shock most educationalists. He regards it as

> learning to speak before one has anything significant to say; and what is taught must have the qualities of being able to be learned without necessarily being understood, and of not being positively hurtful or nonsensical when learned in this way. Or, it may be said, what is taught must be capable of being learned without any previous recognition of ignorance: we do not begin to learn the multiplication tables because it suddenly dawns upon us that we do not know the sum of nine eights, nor the dates of the kings of England because we do not know when Edward I came to the throne: we learn these things at school because we are told to learn them. And further, school-education is without specific orientation; it is not yet concerned with individual talents and aptitudes, and if these show themselves (as they may) the design in school education is not to allow them to take charge. At school we are, quite properly, not permitted to follow our own inclinations.[7]

So much for 'discovery' methods and following the interests of each child!
Actually Oakeshott puts his position more strongly and starkly than

is really either defensible or necessary; for given that school education is all that over two-thirds of the population get at the moment, Oakeshott's view of education as consisting in 'making something of oneself' could only therefore apply to an elite if no account is to be taken, at the school level, of individual aptitude and talent. Also, from the point of view of successful initiation some account must be taken of the inclinations of individuals and of their aptitudes; for motivation is the key to effective initiation. And though it is sheer dogma to assert that learning is only possible if what is to be learnt is closely related to the contingent concerns of the individual, it is equally dogmatic to assert that at school the individual is not allowed to follow his own inclinations, or to deny that a child may learn when Edward I came to the throne because he becomes aware of a gap in his knowledge. Perhaps all that Oakeshott means is that at the school level the content of a curriculum cannot be determined by individual interest or inclination and that at least a 'core' of our common heritage must be transmitted to all. That is reasonable enough. But within this common heritage there is plenty of room for individual aptitudes and it can only be handed on effectively if some account is taken of individual attitudes. Again, though I think that Oakeshott is right, as against many modern educationalists, in insisting that at school much has to be learnt before it can be properly understood or the point of it grasped (for example, moral rules, spelling, reading, poetry), nevertheless it does not follow that there is no place for the type of learning advocated by followers of Dewey or by adherents of 'discovery methods'. There was, after all, some point in Whitehead's polemic against 'inert ideas'.

Vocational education
There are two ways, according to Oakeshott, in which education can branch out after school, which he calls vocational and university education. In vocational education a literature is acquired which is relevant to the performance of some skill or to fitting a man for a specific place in a manner of living. A specific body of knowledge has to be acquired and the individual has to be able to move about within it with ease and confidence and to use it. The history of such a body of knowledge, and the errors and struggles of the past, however instructive, are of no account: what must be handed on is only the current achievement of a civilisation in respect of a skill or practice needed in the contemporary world. No provision need be made for 'teaching people how to be ignorant'.

This account of what is distinctive of technical education is acceptable in a general sort of way, though some of the details are debatable. For instance, it could be argued that Oakeshott has given a delineation of technical training rather than of technical education. Education surely implies some understanding of principles, not just the amassing of information relevant to the practice of a skill or to fitting a man for a place in society. Education also implies some breadth of understanding. On his criterion we would have to say that the Spartans were professionally educated. And surely that is the last thing we would say about them; we would surely say that they were highly trained. We could, however, describe an engineer as educated if he appreciated what was intrinsic to engineering, if he had an understanding of principles and not just a mastery of information relating to engineering, and if he was also capable of appreciating aspects of life other than those intimately connected with engineering.

University education
A university education, according to Oakeshott, has a quite different sort of emphasis; for it is an education in 'languages' rather than in 'literatures'. 'It is concerned not merely to keep an intellectual inheritance intact, but to be continuously recovering what has been lost, restoring what has been neglected, collecting together what has been dissipated, repairing what has been corrupted, reconsidering, reshaping, reorganising, making more intelligible, reissuing and reinvesting.'[8] The direction of study is determined by academic considerations alone, not by extrinsic pressures and demands. The various modes of thought are not taught as literatures to be assimilated but as languages in which different types of exploration can be conducted. What is characteristic of a university education, however, as distinct from that of a graduate school, or a technical college, is that students are given the run of the place where these languages are being used. They do not have to assimilate a body of knowledge to apply for a practical purpose, nor do they have to engage, at the undergraduate level, in research. University teachers, therefore, are not simply frontiersmen on the boundaries of knowledge; they also have to teach from those texts which experience has shown to be most effective in conveying the 'language' of a mode of thought.

Nevertheless, Oakeshott argues, though the main function of a university is to initiate students into the 'language' of a mode of thought, this cannot be done effectively without a study of the appropriate 'literature'. Science as a way of thinking can only be acquired by studying some science; it is no substitute to study some so-called 'scientific method'. Learning to think historically is to be achieved only by observing and following a historian at work on a particular aspect of the past. A 'literature' is studied, therefore, not, as in vocational education, to use for any practical purpose, but as the paradigm of a 'language'.

There is much to be said in favour of Oakeshott's account of university education, especially as a corrective to the views of those who demand that universities should become centres of the 'knowledge industry' and should be concerned mainly with providing the theory to solve the practical problems of the community. But it might be criticised in that he makes a university seem much too like a liberal arts college. In countries where liberal arts colleges have not been separated |from graduate schools and institutes of technology, a university is surely an institution where 'conversations' and teaching are essentially conducted within the context of research. He places too little emphasis on the distinctive character given to such activities by the fact that those who provide most of the talking points are themselves exploring the frontiers of knowledge as well as teaching. On his account a good adult educational settlement, where no one is actively engaged in research, and where no one is a real authority on a subject, would be indistinguishable in its essence from a university. The main difference would be that students do a three-year course – for example, in philosophy or history – for love and without getting a degree for it. Indeed, the absence of a degree would make his notion of contributing to a conversation more applicable; for the fact is that in universities there are sharp-eared men around who listen to the sallies of students and grade and assess them on criteria within one form of thought. This would be very bad form in a real conversation.

PROCESSES OF EDUCATION

Technical and practical knowledge
When Oakeshott addresses himself to the question of how the capital of a civilisation is handed on he makes the same type of distinction as that between a 'language' and a 'literature' but deploys it for a different purpose. He distinguishes technical knowledge which can be formulated in rules, which are, or may be, deliberately learned, remembered and put into practice, and practical knowledge which exists only in use and which cannot be formulated in rules. This does not mean that it is some esoteric sort of knowledge; it only means that the method by which it may be shared and becomes common knowledge is not the method of formulated doctrine. It is what we might call traditional knowledge, and is involved in every kind of activity. Oakeshott's favourite examples, which can be found both in his early article, 'Rationalism in politics',[9] in the *Cambridge Review*, and in his later 'Political education',[10] are cookery, science and politics. There is a body of knowledge in each and recipes for proceeding with the activity; but no one supposes that the knowledge necessary for being a good cook, scientist or politician can be written down in any book. Technique may tell a man what to do, but it is only practice that will tell him how to do it. Techniques, rules, information can be written down; instruction can be given in them; it can even be learned by correspondence. Practical knowledge, on the other hand, can only be shown. It

cannot be taught or learnt; it has to be acquired or imparted. 'It exists only in practice, and the only way to acquire it is by apprenticeship to a master – not because the master can teach it (he cannot), but because it can be acquired only by continuous contact with one who is perpetually practising it.'[11]

Instructing and imparting

In a later lecture delivered at the University of London Institute of Education on 'Learning and teaching'[12] Oakeshott attempts to make more explicit the distinction he has in mind between 'instructing' and 'imparting'. He argues that we carry around with us what we may be said to know in the form of countless abilities, which is an equipment which we possess in terms of what it enables us to do or understand. These abilities are of different kinds and cannot be assimilated to each other – for instance, the ability to understand and to explain cannot be assimilated to the ability to do or to make. Each of these abilities is a conjunction of 'information' and 'judgement'. 'Information' is impersonal and consists of facts that can be written down; it is the answer to the questions 'who? what? where? which? how long? how much?', and so on. It may be useful or useless depending on whether the facts in question are or are not related to a particular skill or ability. Its importance depends on the extent to which it provides rules or rule-like propositions relating to abilities.

There are two ways in which such rules may be related to knowledge. Either they must be known as a condition of being able to perform (for example, the Morse code) or they are rules for assessing performances in terms of correctness or incorrectness (for example, grammatical rules). The latter types of rules are observed in the performance and are capable of being known, they provide the criteria for detecting an incorrect performance, but a knowledge of them is not a condition of a laudable performance. There is also a third type of rule, which may be called principles, which are propositions advanced to explain what is going on in any performance, which supply its 'underlying rationale'. These are never components of the knowledge which constitutes the performance. They belong to the performance of explaining a performance – for instance, in the case of riding a bicycle, the principles of mechanics, in the case of moral conduct Aristotle's doctrine of the mean, which are unrelated either to learning the form of behaviour in question or to a good performance.[13]

There is, then, in all knowledge an ingredient of information which may vary from an indeterminate awareness of facts to rules or rule-like propositions of the first or second sort which inform the skills and abilities in which we carry around what we may be said to know. But this ingredient of information never constitutes the whole of what we know. It must also be partnered by 'judgement'. 'Knowing *how*' must

be added to 'knowing *what*'. This is not merely unspecified in propositions; it is unspecifiable in propositions. It does not and cannot appear
in the form of rules. This is an ingredient of all genuine knowledge and
not a separate kind of knowing specified by an ignorance of rules; for
information has to be used, rules have to be applied, and it does not
itself enable us to interpret it, to decide upon its relevance, to recognise
what action permitted by the rule should, in the circumstances, be
performed. 'For rules are always disjunctive. They specify only an act
or a conclusion of a certain general kind and they never relieve us of
the necessity of advice. And they never yield anything more than
partial explanations: to understand anything as an example of the
operation of a rule is to understand it very imperfectly.'[14]

Judgement, then, is not revealed just in skills like riding a horse or
diagnosing a disease; it is involved also in the practical relationships
between human beings. Maxims and interpersonal rules require
interpretation; where there is a conflict between precepts it cannot be
resolved by the application of other rules. Each individual has a 'style'
of his own which relates to the way in which his judgement is exercised.
'Not to detect a man's style is to have missed three-quarters of the
meaning of his actions and utterances, and not to have acquired a style
is to have shut oneself off from the ability to convey any but the crudest
meanings.[15] In brief, unless a man has developed judgement he has
acquired neither skills nor the different 'languages' characterising the
modes of thought of a civilisation. A mere knowledge of the 'literature', of the information and rules, is insufficient; they may help in
telling us what not to do but they provide no prescriptions for their own
application.

What conclusions, then, does Oakeshott draw for teaching from this
analysis of what has to be passed on? First, that the two components of
knowledge ('information' and 'judgement') can both be communi-
cated and acquired, but not separately. Secondly, that they cannot be
acquired in the same manner. Indeed, Oakeshott confesses that the
distinction which he makes is the result of reflection upon teaching and
learning rather than upon the nature of knowledge. Thus teaching
consists in a twofold activity of 'instructing' (or communicating 'information') and imparting (or communicating 'judgement') and learning
is similarly a twofold activity.

The teacher as instructor is confronted by a pupil who is familiar
with the activity of acquiring information, particularly information of
immediate use. His task is to introduce pupils to facts which have no
immediate significance. He has therefore to decide the part of our
inheritance which has to be transmitted and to make it more readily
accessible by giving it an organisation in which the inertness of its
component facts is modified. 'The organisation provided by an
immediate application to the life of his pupil is spurious; much of the

information he has to convey has no such application and would be corrupted by being turned in this direction.'[16] Dictionaries and éncyclopaedias are no good either; for they are not designed for the purpose of learning. Organisation in terms of 'languages' is altogether too sophisticated. The instructor perforce must settle for more or less arbitrarily designed 'subjects', which compose a curriculum; these are convenient organisations of information, not modes of thought. But they permit facts to reveal their rule-like character as tools to be used in doing, making, or understanding and thus throw off some of their inertness. The teacher as instructor also has to decide on the order in which to present this organisation of facts and to exercise his pupils so that they recognise them in forms other than those in which they were first acquired. Accuracy and readiness to recall are vital in this operation.

In addition to acquiring information from the teacher it is hoped that the pupil is also acquiring judgement. This begins to emerge whenever the pupil perceives that information must be used and perceives the possibility of irrelevance. The organisation of information may help in this development; for the pupil begins to be able to do, make, understand, or explain in the mode of thought which underlies the information. The pupil cannot be instructed how to think in these different ways; it is a by-product of acquiring information and is imparted obliquely in the course of instruction. This can only be done if the information and maxims are constantly related to concrete situations. Also to be imparted are the intellectual virtues that go with judgement – disinterested curiosity, patience, honesty, exactness, industry, concentration and doubt. Most difficult of all for the pupil to acquire is the ability to detect the individual intelligence at work in every utterance and act, the style which each individual brings to his thought and action. 'We may listen to what a man has to say, but unless we overhear in it a mind at work and can detect the idiom of thought, we have understood nothing.'[17]

Judgement is not imparted in the abstract or separately; it is never explicitly learnt and it is known only in practice; but it may be learned in everything that is learned. 'If it is learned, it can never be forgotten, and it does not need to be recollected in order to be enjoyed. It is, indeed often enough, the residue which remains when all else is forgotten; the shadow of lost knowledge.'[18] How, then, is judgement imparted?

It is implanted unobtrusively in the manner in which information is conveyed, in a tone of voice, in the gesture which accompanies instruction, in asides, and oblique utterances, and by example. For 'teaching by example', which is sometimes dismissed as an inferior sort of teaching, generating inflexible knowledge because the rules of what is known remain concealed, is emancipating the pupil from the half-utterance of rules by making him aware of a concrete situation. And in imitating the example he acquires, not merely a model for the particular occasion, but the disposition to recognise everything as an occasion. It is a habit of listening for an individual intelligence at work in every utterance that may be acquired by imitating a teacher who has this habit. And the intellectual virtues may be imparted only by a teacher who really cares about them for their own sake and never stoops to the priggishness of mentioning them. Not the cry, but the rising of the wild duck impels the flock to follow him in flight.[19]

THE THESIS AS A CONCEPTUAL TRUTH OR AS AN EMPIRICAL GENERALISATION

Oakeshott's distinction between 'instructing' and 'imparting' is obviously a very important one, but the details of it are not altogether clear. So it is necessary to probe a bit further into it. He seems to maintain, first, that things like judgement, taste and discernment can only be imparted; they can never be the result of mere instruction. Information and rules, on the other hand, are fit material only for instruction. Secondly, 'imparting', in Oakeshott's view, must involve the example of the teacher; things like 'judgement' can only be 'shown', and this is how they are picked up. The rulebook will not do, because the rules have to be applied, and we can only learn to apply them by working with somebody who knows how to apply them.

The first part of this thesis seems to be partly a *conceptual* truth in that 'impart' rather than 'instruct' is the word which we use when we wish to indicate that something has been successfully learnt from a teacher, as well as when we wish also to suggest some sort of mystery about how this has been accomplished. 'Impart', in other words, is what Ryle calls an 'achievement' word.[20] It implies, surely, not necessarily that the teacher has been engaged in some activity additional to instructing but that he has somehow achieved success in his task. Thus, contrary to Oakeshott's thesis, information or rules can be imparted, as well as judgement and discernment. As, however, it is desirable that information should be used and rules applied, judgement would usually be regarded as a criterion of success, rather than the mere acquisition of information. The pupil should emerge with judgement and discernment rather than just be stuffed with 'inert' ideas. It is, therefore, not surprising that Oakeshott associates 'imparting' with 'judgement'; for this is the word which we use when we wish to point to the teacher's success. But it is not the case that only judgement can be imparted. It is merely a contingent fact that we do not regard the mere passing-on of information as sufficiently important to grace it often with a 'success' word.

But is it also true – and this, too, might be a conceptual truth or it might be an empirical generalisation – that such successful results only occur when the teacher 'shows' or exemplifies the proper performance? Must there be some sort of mystery about the transaction which the term 'impart' also suggests? Could not, or cannot, mere instruction be sufficient? This is a much more complicated question to answer; for Oakeshott maintains that all passing-on of knowledge and skill must involve the imparting of judgement if it is to be successful. But to maintain such a general thesis he uses the word 'judgement' in several different ways, at least three of which must be distinguished.

(1) There is, first of all, a general sense of 'judgement' used by idealist philosophers such as Bradley to speak of any situation in which a concept or rule is applied to a particular case. Thus recognising something as red or as a cat or as a breach of the Highway Code involves 'judgement' in this sense, just as much as recognising someone who is in disguise or determining whether someone was driving with due care and precaution. Does 'judgement' in this very general sense have to be imparted by processes such as imitation or identification in which acts or noises are copied or attitudes, interests and wants are 'taken in' from the example of a teacher?

The answer is that, in this sense of judgement, examples are useful for learning but not necessarily essential. To be able to perceive or think is to be able to use concepts, and learning a concept involves both learning the rule which binds together the instances and learning by examples what counts as an instance. That is why a colour-blind man could not have a full concept of 'red'. But this process of producing an example to teach a concept or a rule is the most typical case of *instruction* If we say 'cat' to a child and point to the animal in question that is a case of instruction. If we say later that 'the cat is on the mat' and again point, that again is a piece of instruction. If the instruction is successful, either in the sense that the child can go on to use the words correctly in this and in different situations, or in the sense that he remembers the piece of information, then we might say that we had taught the child a concept or imparted some knowledge to him. Judgement in its most general idealist sense would be involved; but though, at some stage, the use of examples would be necessary, the example of the teacher would not. After all, a great deal of instruction of this sort can be carried out by teaching machines.

Now 'judgement' of the idealist sort is obviously something much more mundane than the 'judgement' of a judge, and situations can be controlled and structured in such a way that the learner can grasp the concept by instruction. He has, of course, to be brought to grasp the rules involved; but instructions can be formalised for bringing students of average intelligence to grasp such rules. Example, as distinct from examples, only becomes important when something approximating to a skill is involved. It might be argued that in the early stages of learning an embryonic sort of skill is involved; for rules and concepts at this stage are necessarily presented in unstructured and unfamiliar types of situations where the child has to discriminate between possible types of application. Even in learning 'blue', for instance, the child has to grasp that this is an information-conveying type of word rather than an order, and that it is a colour-word within the general class of information-conveying types of word. Unless he has picked up a lot about the use of language from the example of his parents he will not be in a position to benefit from instruction by examples. Once he has become a language-user instruction can accomplish a lot merely by examples because he has 'picked up' the general skills involved in using language in different ways by following the example of others. This may well be true; but what it also shows is that there is a great deal of 'judgement' in the idealist sense which can be learnt by instruction once the general skill of using a language has been acquired.

(2) The general skill of using a language may exemplify a second and more specific sense of 'judgement', the paradigm case of which is the type of task performed by a judge. He is faced by a complex situation where many rules might apply to a set of facts and he has to determine which rule does apply. Judgement of a similar sort is involved in diagnosis, in tact, in deciding which golf club to use, or in dealing with non-routine types of situation in war, business and politics. This is surely the type of situation with which the term 'judgement' is usually associated.

'Judgement', in Oakeshott's thesis, is above all a term of approval. But we do not give a person a merit mark for judgement in the first sense – that is, if he recognises an obvious breach of the Highway Code or if he straightaway follows some instructions correctly for getting to Piccadilly. If he failed in such elementary applications of rules or use of information we might think him a fool. But we certainly would not praise him particularly if he was successful or ascribe judgement to him. It may well be the case that the difference between 'judgement' in the first and second senses is a difference in degree; it may well be the case also that judgement in the first idealist sense is only possible if some skill has been mastered which once involved judgement in the second sense. But the fact is that we do not normally use the word 'judgement' for straightforward cases of applying rules or using information. We reserve it for the special cases where applying rules or interpreting information presents a problem.

Could people only learn judgement in this second value-laden sense by serving their apprenticeship under somebody who already has it? That this is the only way in which it could be learnt seems to be the burden of Oakeshott's political and educational writings, in which he usually contrasts this way of picking it up with formalised instruction or the use of manuals and guides. No doubt some kind of apprenticeship system is the most effective and the quickest way of learning judgement of this sort. But it is questionable whether it is the only way. Oakeshott has a contempt for self-made men; but though they may learn judgement the hard way, it has to be demonstrated that they cannot learn it on their own, which seems to be his thesis. Oakeshott also has a contempt for method; yet method at least provides canons laying down what should not be done; it provides boundary fences within which the learner can try out things for himself. And here we come to the core of the matter, which is insufficiently emphasised in all Oakeshott's writings: *practice*, in which the learner methodically works at some task until he has more or less mastered it and is able to rest on a solid basis of habit in tackling some novel situation. Of course what we call 'training' usually involves practice under the supervision of some skilled performer. But it is a disputable empirical thesis that this is the only way to develop skill and judgement. Who, after all, was the master whose philosophical 'judgement' rubbed off on Socrates?

Of course those who are self-taught must learn 'judgement' in the first idealist sense from others; they have to learn to speak and to apply rules in paradigm situations before they can carry on on their own; they have to be familiar with a literature from which problems or incoherences arise which puzzle them. But, given such a start, practice, intelligence and method can take a man a very long way more or less on his own. Dewey's account of the development of critical thinking certainly pays too little attention to the role of the teacher as a paradigm of a form of thinking; it is *too* biased in favour of the do-it-yourself ideology of the frontier. But it would be odd if this rationalistic type of account applied to *no* cases in which people gradually learned to think for themselves and if *all* people who were more or less self-taught necessarily lacked judgement. Could it not be the case, too, that a man who was not a very good philosopher or scientist himself might be very good at initiating others in the early stages? He might have the ability to exhibit and convey to others the essentials of a form of thought in a crude but exciting way. He might lack the judgement to progress very far with it himself, to be an acknowledged master; but he might be very good at initiating others at the undergraduate level.

Oakeshott's emphasis, too, on picking up a skill by watching a master overlooks a very common learning situation that is not to be despised – that in which a learner practises a skill with a coach who is not himself particularly proficient at the skill in question. Some of the best teachers of golf or cricket, for instance, are not themselves superlative performers. What they have mastered is the art of commenting on and encouraging the performances of others. And they often do this by the reiteration of rules which are anathema to Oakeshott. They say things like 'Keep your right elbow in' or 'Don't hit from the top of the swing'. The performer gradually improves in response to such discerning instructions. There are, perhaps, many who learn much better by imitation which lacks such rule-ridden self-consciousness; but on the other hand, others may not be particularly imitative and may learn better if coached by one who knows what a good performance looks like without himself being a superlative performer. Could it not be that Oakeshott's thesis about learning by example is merely a generalisation of his own favoured way of learning? Oakeshott produces no empirical evidence for his general thesis. But, perhaps, like Hobbes he reached it by reading in himself 'not this or that particular man; but mankind'.

Perhaps Oakeshott conflates under the general heading of 'teaching by example' two features of a situation which do not always go together. There is first of all that of the exhibition of the performance in question by the teacher and there is secondly the imparting of a skill or judgement not just by examples but by on-the-spot correction of the pupil's efforts towards mastery of it. It is conceivable that a learner could achieve considerable expertise in some skill like golf or shooting without reliance on either aspect of such an apprenticeship situation. For this would be a situation where the goal is more or less unambiguous and skill in hitting a target could be achieved by trial and error and constant practice. But in fields like that of the law or politics, where the notion of an overall 'goal' is rather out of place and where what constitutes success in a given case depends upon multiple criteria, it is almost inconceivable that a person could become proficient without one or other aspect of the apprenticeship system being present. For as Aristotle put it 'the decision lies with perception'. There may be ninety-nine ways of going wrong and only one way of going right. If judgements of this sort could be formalised in rules there would be no need to have judges for applying the rules of a legal system. A man could not, in such situations, learn 'judgement' on his own because he could never know what was constitutive of success. In shooting or golf, on the other hand, he might do this because he would know that success consisted in hitting the bird or getting the ball into the hole in as few shots as possible. It is only if an activity like politics is viewed as the pursuit of an overall end such as power that the do-it-yourself form of learning begins to look appropriate. Hence Oakeshott's strictures on books like Machiavelli's *The Prince* and on the general conception of politics as the taking of means to independently premeditated ends.

The upshot of this analysis would be, then, that in so far as an activity approximates to a skill which could be said to be 'goal-directed' in a fairly determinate way, there would be a correspondingly open possibility of do-it-yourself methods of learning, given a preliminary period of initiation into the rudiments of the activity. In so far, however, as 'success' in an activity is impossible to characterise without concrete interpretations or implementations of general principles, the possibility of do-it-yourself methods would become correspondingly more remote. But though apprenticeship would be necessary for the attainment of skill or judgement in such complex activities it need not take the form of learning from the example of the master; it might be sufficient for the master to correct the performances of his pupils on the spot. One of the best swimming coaches in recent times was a man who could not swim.

(3) Oakeshott also refers on occasions to a third sort of thing, the 'style' of the individual performer. By this he means to draw attention not just to individual acts of judgement in the second sense but to the individual intelligence at work in every utterance and performance. It is necessarily the case that in so far as this can be passed on it must involve example; for as it is, by definition, individual to the person concerned, comprising a characteristic manner of thinking and acting, it would have to be shown to be both detected and imparted.

When talking about 'style' Oakeshott seems to conflate together the possibility of detecting it in another and the possibility of acquiring it from another. But the two do not necessarily go together. There are many philosophers of discernment who can detect Wittgenstein's characteristic 'style' of philosophy; but, though their own mastery of the 'language' might lead them to recognise the importance of many of his insights, they might well shudder at the 'style' with which they were delivered. Others, however, might admire the performance as a whole and might model themselves on it – mannerisms and all. This brings out that 'style' for Oakeshott is a term of approval which is associated only with desirable traits. But much of a person's 'style' may be an unnecessary and perhaps trivial or distracting adornment. There was a time when one could almost tell where an English philosopher was trained by observing the mannerisms and gestures which had been imparted to him!

Oakeshott, I feel sure, would deplore too much absorption of the 'style' of another. For that would be inconsistent with his insistence that 'making something of ourselves' is an important aspect of education. Presumably he means that it is judgement in the second sense, which is to be acquired from masters of the different languages; their individual style (including its superflous idiosyncrasies) is to be 'detected' and admired but not slavishly copied.

When Oakeshott speaks about the imparting of judgement his own style of writing intimates somehow that we are confronted with a mystery. Indeed he perhaps chooses the word 'impart' because of its association with recondite matters. He cites no mundane empirical studies of apprenticeship and the transmission of skills; he indulges in no speculation about the psychological processes involved. Theories about roles, imitation, or identification are never mentioned. He leads his readers to the uncharted region between the logical and psychological and there he leaves them. *Omne ignotum pro magnifico*.

There are others, however, for whom a mystery is not something that is to be hinted at and enjoyed, especially when it is alleged to pervade every situation in which a new generation is being initiated into skill, taste and judgement. On the contrary it provides a splendid occasion to satisfy all those rationalistic yearnings for clarity and problem-solving that Oakeshott so deeply deplores. Any mundane fellow who is set on exploring this uncharted region will first of all have to map the concepts which criss-cross the region. He will then need a spade to dig into psychological and sociological theories in order to unearth some relevant generalisations about social learning. My guess is that he will not find himself working alone but will find that he is helping to open up a region which will prove to be one of the most fertile for the growth of educational theory during the next decade. More understanding of these apprenticeship situations may dispel the mystery a bit, but not the wonder. It may even help us to teach a bit better.

MORAL EDUCATION

Oakeshott's account of moral education depends largely on the distinction which he makes between the 'habit of affection and behaviour' of the person brought up in a settled tradition and the 'reflective morality' of the person brought up to pursue ideals and to implement principles. It depends, too, on the rather idiosyncratic understanding which he has of 'principles' and of the lack of connection between them and behaviour. On the one hand he argues[21] that there is (or perhaps was) a form of moral life which consists in a 'habit of affection and behaviour'. People do not reflect upon alternative courses of action and make choices determined by principles or ideals; they simply follow unreflectively the tradition in which they have been brought up. They acquire this in the way in which they learn to speak their mother tongue, by living with others who practise this morality. No doubt what they learn can be formulated in rules; but there is no need for it to be. People can learn to speak grammatically without their having also to be able to formulate rules of grammar. This sort of education, therefore, gives people the power to act appropriately without hesitation in a whole range of situations; but it does not give them the ability to explain or defend their actions as emanations of moral principles. A man has acquired what this type of education can teach him when his moral dispositions are inseparably connected with his *amour propre*. This form of behaviour, though traditional, is not fixed; for it evolves in the way in which a living language evolves.

On the other hand there is reflective morality, which is determined not by a habit of behaviour but by the reflective application of a moral criterion. It takes the form either of the self-conscious pursuit of moral ideals or of the reflective observance of moral rules. A man must first formulate his rule of life or his ideal in words; he must also have the ability to defend these formulated aspirations against criticism. And, thirdly, he must learn to apply them in current situations in life and problem-solving behaviour. Moral education, therefore, must consist first of all in the detection and appreciation of ideals and principles. Secondly, there must be training in the art of their intellectual man-agement and thirdly, training in the art of their application to concrete circumstances. The danger of this form of morality is that uncertainty in action is more or less proportionate to certainty in thinking about these ideals; moral reflection may undermine moral habit. It will make people miserable because of its demand for perfection and will suffer from inelasticity and imperviousness to change.

Oakeshott realises, of course, that these two sorts of morality are really 'ideal types'. In most actual moralities there is a blend of the two. His concern is to attack a way of life in which the latter rather than the former type of morality predominates.

Before discussing the dichotomy it is necessary to clarify Oakeshott's conception of 'principles'. He regards them as 'abstracts' of practice. His frequent use of the word 'ideology' in this context is significant; for Oakeshott regards principles as being somehow spuri-ous in relation to justification and, causally speaking, as by-products of activity. Indeed I think that it is his relativistic conviction that they cannot be justified that leads him to speak of them as 'explaining' conduct in the above passage in which he contrasts 'principles' with rules of correctness implicit in conduct as well as in the grammar of a language. He exemplifies Aristotle's doctrine of the mean in the case of conduct being on a par with the principles of mechanics in the case of riding a bicycle.

There may be something rather special about the status of Aris-totle's doctrine of the mean. But, whatever one makes of Aristotle's doctrine, this is really a very odd use of 'principle' in the run-of-the-mill moral case. When speaking of principles Oakeshott always quotes something pretty abstract like 'natural rights' or 'justice', but surely, in the moral sphere, all we mean by a 'principle' is something that provides backing to a rule or which makes reasons relevant. Whether or not fundamental principles such as 'justice' or 'the minimisation of avoidable suffering' can themselves be justified is a very complicated question;[22] but certainly the relationship between rules of conduct and principles is one of justification. In a moral context a principle just *is* a higher-order rule that is appealed to when justification is required for one at a lower order. Thus if someone like Mill claims that divorce is wrong if the married couple have children, because of the probable suffering that it will cause them, then the avoidance of suffering is functioning as a principle. 'Judgement' is, of course, needed in order to apply such a principle; for what counts as suffering in a particular case and whose suffering is to be given most weight? Much of what Oakeshott says about 'judgement' is more pertinent to the application of principles. But it is his bizarre account of them that leads him to say that an appeal to them is a rationalist aberration. Indeed his own account even of 'practical' or 'traditional' knowledge is unintelligible without assuming a background of principles; for without such a background how are any reasons for action relevant? Oakeshott's account of the politician keeping the ship of state on an even keel and dealing with 'incoherences' which arise in a developing tradition presupposes not only that 'coherence' is good (whatever this amounts to in practice!) but also that considerations relating to security and stability are relevant. And if *salus populi suprema lex* is not a 'principle' I do not know what is.

Oakeshott, too, seems to think that principles are really 'abstracts' from practices, whereas he caricatures rationalists as thinking that they are rules that are formulated as guides to practice. But why should they be either? Some principles, for instance, might be presuppositions of a practice. They need not be formulated beforehand by those who indulge in it, neither need they be abstracts from it. The principle, for instance, that truth matters need not be formulated beforehand by people discussing some scientific problem. It need only be appealed to if a participant in the discussion starts introducing irrelevant personal remarks or disregarding some evidence. Neither is it necessarily an 'abstract' of the practice of discussion; for such a discussion would surely be unintelligible unless the participants were already committed to it. For they have to conceive the situation in a certain way in order to make it a practice of this determinate sort. In a similar way the concern for health is a presupposition of, not an abstract from, the practice of medicine. There is therefore a sense in which Oakeshott's account of 'practices' is as inadequate as his account of 'principles'.

To probe further into the relationship between principles and practices would take us too far away from Oakeshott's philosophy of education. It must also be remarked that though Oakeshott's ideal types of morality provide two fascinating models that might have had application to classes of people within our society at some distant time in the past, they have little application to adults in modern industrial societies in the West. This is admitted by Oakeshott when he claims that nowadays the two are blended and that his main purpose is to attack a way of life which includes too much of the reflective and too little of the traditional style of behaviour.

From the point of view of moral education, however, both his dichotomy and his emphasis on tradition are instructive, as I have argued elsewhere.[23] Given that we live in a changing society with a fair degree of differentiation at a certain level in moral standards, young people are bound to be forced to reflect from time to time on where they stand. They have, therefore, to develop the elements of what Oakeshott calls a reflective morality, though his account of it, with the bizarre role accorded to principles in it, would have to be modified. But, for a variety of reasons, it is out of the question for young children to acquire such a morality until they pass out of what Piaget calls the 'transcendental stage' of moral judgement. At an early age, therefore, their morality will have to approximate to Oakeshott's 'habit of affection and behaviour'. The crucial task of moral education is to initiate them into this in such a way that they can gradually come to grasp the principles underlying what they have picked up from their parents and teachers, so that they will be able to act with understanding and adapt their practice to moral situations, make sensible choices and perhaps even challenge some practices as no longer defensible. The palace of reason has to be entered by the courtyard of habit. There are too many 'progressive' educators and parents who place too little emphasis on the enormous importance of habit and tradition in moral education. Oakeshott's brilliant sketch of traditional morality is a healthy corrective to such rationalistic excesses.

CONCLUSION

It is a recurrent theme in Oakeshott's writings that a man who is skilled at something such as cooking may not have the additional skill of being able to make explicit what he is about. Oakeshott himself provides a clear case of a person who combines both sorts of gifts. He is a gifted teacher and administrator whose unpretentious concern both for his subject and for his students is immanent in everything that he does. And I have never known a man with such contempt for conscience discharge his duties so conscientiously. So when he reflects and writes, one feels that it is a genuine reflection of his experience and view of the world. Above all writers on politics and education today he has a style, an idiom of his own, and this is inseparable from his conduct of affairs. There is nothing second-hand or spurious about it or him. One may not agree with him – or, to put it more accurately, one agrees with him so much at first that it is particularly infuriating when he proceeds to what one thinks is the wrong conclusion! But he is there, all of a piece, to remind us perhaps of values that we are in danger of forgetting in the present gimmickry which passes for politics and in the present escalation of education, with its emphasis on equality rather than quality.

It has not been until recently the fashion for university teachers outside education departments to write much about education. They thought they knew about it, of course; for are they not teachers themselves and have they not been to school? But their reflections about it were about as informed as a farmer's reflections about the weather. Recently, however, since it has been widely recognised that education is both an investment for the community and a means of social ascent for the individual, there have been many academics who have given forth on the subject of the organisation and distribution of education. Oakeshott, however, is one of the few who have consistently reflected and written on what the business is really about. Indeed, he confesses that his views about knowledge derive from his reflections on teaching. And when he writes about education it is manifest that he knows what it is about. He knows too that matters of organisation and distribution are of secondary importance compared with the heart of the matter – the living contact between a teacher and his pupils. This essay has only attempted to convey the main contours of his thought. There have, too, been criticisms and queries – mainly on points of detail. But what cannot be adquately conveyed in such an abstract of a way of thinking is the overall impression of an extremely civilised man writing with acuteness, elegance and conviction about a matter which is of no small account – the passing on of a civilisation.

REFERENCES: CHAPTER 6

1 See Benn, S.I., and Peters, R.S., *Social Principles and the Democratic State* (London: Allen & Unwin, 1958), pp. 312–18.
2 Oakeshott, M., 'The study of politics in a university', in *Rationalism in Politics and Other Essays* (London: Methuen, 1962), p. 304.
3 ibid., p. 304.
4 loc. cit.
5 ibid., p. 308
6 ibid., p. 305.
7 ibid., p. 306.
8 ibid., p. 310.
9 Oakeshott, M., reprinted in *Rationalism in Politics and Other Essays*, pp. 8–11.
10 Also reprinted in ibid., pp. 119–23.
11 ibid., p. 11
12 Published in Peters, R.S. (ed.), *The Concept of Education* (London: Routledge & Kegan Paul, 1966).
13 ibid., p. 166.
14 ibid., p. 168.
15 ibid., p. 169.
16 ibid., p. 171.
17 ibid., p. 174.
18 ibid., p. 175.
19 ibid., p. 175.
20 See Ryle, G., *The Concept of Mind* (London: Hutchinson, 1949), pp. 149–53.

21 See 'The Tower of Babel', in *Rationalism in Politics and Other Essays*, pp. 61–70.
22 See Peters, R.S., *Ethics and Education* (London: Allen & Unwin, 1965), chs III–VIII.
23 See Peters, R.S., 'The paradox of moral education', in Niblett, W.R. (ed.), *Moral Education in a Changing Society* (London: Faber, 1963); reprinted in Peters, R.S., *Psychology and Ethical Development* (London: Allen & Unwin, 1974).

Part Three

Interdisciplinary Critiques

Chapter 7

The Place of Kohlberg's Theory in Moral Education*

A SKINNERIAN SCENARIO

Let me start with a thumb-nail sketch of B.F. Skinner's diagnosis of our moral malaise and the contours of its cure. In his view we have a large-scale problem of survival – not just economic but social as well. The fabric of society is threatened by violence, greed, theft, drug addiction, pollution and so on. Largely to blame are our thoroughly inefficient and superstitious ways of bringing up the young. Encouraged by the antiquated belief in our autonomy we make appeals to reason. These are supported by a mixture of permissiveness and punitive measures. Permissiveness only lays the child open to haphazard influences other than those of parents and teachers and punishment has been shown to be counter-productive in relation to learning.

The only scientifically supported alternative to our amateurish tinkering with the problem is the shaping of behaviour along socially desirable lines by a combination of systematic instruction in morals and modelling backed up by positive reinforcements. The social environment must be controlled and designed to encourage co-operative and socially useful forms of behaviour. Rules and practices that are essential to social survival must be singled out and instilled in the young by Skinnerian techniques. His recipe for salvation has much in common with the type of moral education practised in the Soviet Union as described by Bronfenbrenner in his *Two Worlds of Childhood*.[1]

There are obvious moral objections to such a programme which I will not labour. Most of us, though perhaps believing autonomy to be rather an overworked virtue, would not dismiss it as a relic of the belief in a little man within a man; we would resist his attack on freedom and human dignity and the lack of respect for persons shown by both; and we might be sceptical at the superior value placed on happiness in the fancy dress of positive reinforcement. I propose to pass by such criticisms as too obvious to need development and to turn to the sort of

*This essay was first presented as a paper at an international conference on moral education and moral development held at Leicester University, 19–26 August 1977.

psychological criticisms that might be made by someone like Kohlberg as a way of introducing his theory. I shall, however, return to Skinner's type of approach; for, as I shall hope to show, there are elements in it which are necessary supplements to Kohlberg's own approach.

KOHLBERG'S CRITICISMS

(1) Kohlberg claims, first of all, that learning theorists have produced no positive evidence of the influence of early forms of habit training on adult behaviour.[2] Most of the evidence is negative – for example, from studies of exposure to boy scouts, Sunday school, and so on, and of early parental training in habits such as punctuality and neatness.[3] But Skinner would be unimpressed by such vague findings; for the techniques used were not made explicit, neither was there any systematic control of the patterns of reinforcement.

(2) Of more substance would be Kohlberg's claim that this represents a 'bag of virtues' approach, an attempt systematically to instil in the young socially important virtues such as honesty and co-operation, which he claims are situation-specific and not enduring traits of character. They depend very much on the continued presence of reinforcing agencies and are likely to collapse when those are absent. Kohlberg suggests that there is some evidence that they are stable if supported either by principles or by ego-strength or by strength of will. The trouble about this criticism is that it is based on the controversial Hartshorne–May inquiry which dealt with a very limited number of virtues and, as I have argued elsewhere,[4] virtues are not all of a piece. Of particular importance is the fact that some are also motives for action, whereas others are not. Honesty, tidiness and punctuality, for instance, are not motives; they have no obvious reason for action built into them. It is not therefore surprising that they tend to be situation-specific depending upon what further reasons there may be for conforming to them, including the probability of rewards and punishment, approval and disapproval. Virtues like these are to be contrasted with gratitude, prudence and compassion which are also motives. They contain within themselves reasons for action which make them less strongly dependent on contextual considerations. Of course people may not act out of them because they deem some other feature of the situation to be more important. But if by 'important' is meant morally important this does not show that they are context-dependent. For virtues, as well as rules and principles, must be guarded by an 'other things being equal' clause. And other things are not equal if there is a conflict-of-duties situation.

There is another sense in which virtues are context-dependent which applies equally, if not more strongly, to the principles in which Kohlberg puts his trust. This is connected with variations of interpretation as to what is to *count* as stealing, cheating, dishonesty, and the like. But as there are notorious difficulties about what is to count as justice (does one estimate it on the basis of need or merit, for instance?), or what is to count as people's interests, this type of difficulty has not to be faced only by those who want to make room for a bag of virtues in morality in general and moral education in particular, to supplement the emphasis which Kohlberg places on principles.

(3) Kohlberg's third and more fundamental criticism would be that Skinner is concerned only with moral learning, not with moral development. His techniques would have the effect of arresting people at the stage of conventional morality, without encouraging them to pass to the stage of principled morality.

KOHLBERG'S PROGRESSION

(1) Logical stages
Kohlberg's defence of a principled morality and of the supreme importance of cognitive factors is too well known to require exposition. I have worries about it on at least two scores. First, I think that it has difficulties internal to it. Secondly, because of the eloquence and voluminousness with which he has expounded it, it is very easy for the unsophisticated reader to be carried away and to think that the main ingredients of moral development have been revealed. Some constructive comment is therefore called for to protect Kohlberg against his own persuasiveness. For he would be the first to admit that his theory covers only part of the process of moral development.

My first batch of worries relates to the progression from stage to stage. I am not competent enough in empirical psychology to comment on the reliability and validity of the devices by means of which Kohlberg claims to have established them, as have Kurtines and Greif.[5] Neither can I do more than note with interest Gibbs's[6] recent contention that Kohlberg's first four stages satisfy Piaget-type criteria of development but that the last two stages do not. My worry is more deep-seated; for Kohlberg claims that the stages form a hierarchical logical sequence, which implies that they logically must occur in the order which research has revealed them to occur.

If this were true the need for extensive research about the order of stages would seem superfluous; for they could be arrived at by reflection. To take a parallel, Piaget, after elaborate investigation of children, demonstrated the progression from concrete operations to formal operations. But Plato, in his brilliant allegory of the ascent from the Cave, had already demonstrated this over two thousand years ago on the basis of a mixture of reflection and imagination. Similarly, in the moral sphere, it is difficult to see how an autonomous type of morality could precede a conventional one; for unless a child has had some prior introduction to rule-following and knows, from the inside, what it is to apply rules to his conduct, the notion of accepting or rejecting rules for himself would scarcely seem intelligible. Kant's heteronomy and autonomy, which are the intellectual ancestors of Piaget's and Kohlberg's stages, were not postulated as the result of empirical investigation.

The trouble is, however, that this kind of conceptual truth does not manifestly apply to the details of Kohlberg's progression, even though he appeals to the logical hierarchy of stages to explain their cultural invariance. I can see no kind of logical necessity in the claim that the 'good boy morality' of the peer group must precede a morality more dependent on the approval of authorities, for instance, in stages three and four. There may be some kind of necessity for this, connected with the logical order of the concepts concerned; but Kohlberg has not made explicit what it is any more than he has made explicit, at stages one and two, why children must conceive of rules as connected with punishment before they see them as connected with rewards. I have raised this query before and still await Kohlberg's detailed demonstration of the alleged logical necessity.

Then there are stages five and six, about which so little can be said because there are so few case-studies of individuals who have reached them. About these stages I would be inclined to generalise Gibbs's thesis in that, once a person has achieved some kind of autonomy, and can reflect in a principled kind of way on rules, I can see no logical reason why he should not come up with any type of ethical position, rather than passing from a system characterised by an ideal order to one characterised by abstract principles. Whether reflective people embody their principles in ideal constructions like Hobbes's *Leviathan* or Rousseau's *Social Contract* or whether, like Sidgwick and Price, they formulate their principles in a more mundane, abstract manner seems more to do with their imaginative and literary gifts than with their level of moral reasoning. And anyway, what application has the notion of level of moral reasoning to those who have reached a stage at which they keenly dispute the priority of each other's principles? And what place are we to accord to an acute and abstract-minded sceptic such as David Hume who argued that morals depend not on rational principles but on disinterested passions?

My scepticism about the logical order of Kohlberg's stages, together with Gibbs's claims about the unsatisfactoriness of stages five and six, and my own failure to see why reflection at the post-conventional stages, should not lead to a pluralism of ethical positions, combine to attract me to Bronfenbrenner's and Garbarino's socialisation model[7] in which there are three stages resulting from the interaction between maturing capacities and motivations of the child on the one hand and particular characteristics of his sociocultural milieu on the other. At the bottom is the amoral pattern with some primary hedonic principle of organisation such as self-interest or self-satisfaction. The second level includes all patterns of morality having as their dominant characteristic allegiance and orientation to some system of social agents. These include authority, peer and collective orientations. These are alternatives and may exist within and across cultures. They need not occur in any particular order in an individual. At the third level values, principles and ideas are the directing forces. This is Kohlberg's stages five and six without the emphasis on the principle of justice. For this level to emerge a very special set of social conditions is required.

(2) Cognitive stimulation
My other worry about the progression from stage to stage relates to the distinction that Kohlberg makes between 'teaching' and 'cognitive stimulation'. He holds that the *content* of moral rules can be taught but the attitude to them characteristic of the various stages cannot. It is a matter of the child's interaction with the social environment aided by 'cognitive stimulation'. But as he takes Socrates' method of bringing the young to grasp principles as a method of cognitive stimulation he is obviously employing a very narrow concept of 'teaching'; for in any straightforward sense Socrates was teaching the slave in *Meno* all right, even though he was not telling him anything. By 'teaching' he seems to mean direct instruction and it is obvious enough why the view of rules that characterises the different stages could not be imparted in this way. For it is not a memory task nor the acquisition of a skill. The learner has to catch on; the penny has to drop. And this comes about by being put in the way of plenty of examples with appropriate stimulation from others – for instance – in questioning, role-playing, and so on. What is not clear, however, is what else might be cognitively stimulating. Kohlberg claims that the peer-group – especially those at a slightly higher level – is an important source of cognitive stimulation. But is the modelling that goes on in such groups as well as the discussion and role-playing a source of such stimulation? Does exposure to TV help? And so on. I find the concept of 'cognitive stimulation' reasonably staightforward when it is used to describe a group of methods for getting a child to grasp a principle like that of conservation in Piagetian experiments. But I do not find it very easy to pin down in the contexts in which children acquire different orientations to rules, except, of course, in the experiments done with children under controlled conditions by Turiel and Rest.[8]

THE AFFECTIVE ASPECTS OF MORALITY

The crown of Kohlberg's moral system is the principle of justice. Considering the importance which he attaches to it, he is very elusive in his treatment of it. Sometimes it appears in the skeleton form of Hare's

prescriptivity and universalisability. At other times it is fleshed out
with references to freedom and human welfare. Sometimes reciprocity
and respect for persons are thrown in. And so on. But I do not want to
enter into details of Kohlbergian exegesis; I want rather to make two
points about his treatment which open up a whole vista of moral
development with which his system does not deal, namely, the affective aspects of development.

When Kohlberg talks of the principle of justice, it is not clear
whether he has in mind the very formal principle that no distinctions
should be made unless there are relevant differences or more concrete
versions of it in distributive or commutative justice. But any application of this principle must involve a love of consistency and a hatred of
arbitrariness. What is the developmental history of this sense of justice? Kohlberg, like Piaget, postulates a striving for 'equilibration'
which leads children to assimilate and accommodate. This is the main
motivation for development. I have elsewhere[9] tried to show that this
biological metaphor is unnecessary. What Piaget is talking about is the
striving for consistency. This may be necessary but it surely is not
sufficient when we are dealing with the motivational side of moral
development and not just with intellectual development. What is
missing?

(1) Consideration for others

The clue to what is missing can be found, I think, by returning to the
principle of justice. For justice is, as it were, the principle of principles,
which may have led Kohlberg to have accorded it such pre-eminence.
In its minimal form of impartiality it holds that no exceptions are to be
made to a principle unless there are relevant grounds. In its more
full-blooded form it demands impartial consideration of people's
claims and interests. The point is that it cannot be employed unless
something *else* of value is at stake. For unless there is some other
criterion of value how do we determine relevance? Questions of justice, too, simply do not arise unless something of value has to be
distributed or exchanged. Usually what is at stake is people's welfare
or interests. It is no accident that occasionally Kohlberg slips in some
reference to human welfare when he talks about his higher stages. So
we have at least one more fundamental principle in the system – the
consideration of people's interests. (I will not tease Kohlberg by calling
it the virtue of benevolence!) I happen to think that this fundamental
principle is as important in morality as the principle of justice. Yet
there is no proper genetic account of it in either Piaget or Kohlberg,
presumably because of their Kantian ancestry. It is true that Piaget
gives an ingenious account, in terms of role-taking, of how the
development of concrete operations coincides with the ability to take
the point of view of another. But he never shows why a child should

care about the other whose point of view he can take. And this is what requires explanation. The question is whether some account can be given of it which is a congenial supplement to the Piaget–Kohlberg story.

McPhail's *Lifeline* programme[10] makes caring for others the pivotal point of its material. But he was concerned with devising suitable teaching material for adolescents, not with a developmental progression. Indeed his emphasis on the rewarding character of this type of behaviour to the individual who practises it suggests that he is catering for those not far advanced in Kohlberg's stages. But he is surely right in emphasising 'consideration for the needs, feelings and interests of others' in morality even if he rather underplays the importance of more rational principles such as justice.

But what of the developmental aspect of this principle with which neither McPhail nor Kohlberg deals? Recently Martin Hoffman has suggested a developmental theory of altruism which is consistent with Piagetian principles.[11] As his theory may be unfamiliar to many I will sketch its rough outlines. His assumption is that man is innately capable of both egoistic and altruistic motivation and his aim is to propose a theory of how the latter may develop in the individual. The basis of his theory is the human capacity to experience the inner state of others who are not in the same situation. It begins with empathy, the involuntary experiencing of another's emotional state. He suggests classical conditioning paradigms to explain this, either in terms of early transfer of tension from the caretaker to the child, or in terms of the unpleasant affect accompanying one's own painful past experiences which is evoked by another person's distress cues which resemble the stimuli associated with the observer's own experiences. These explanations are highly controversial. Irene Sebastian and Thomas Wren, for instance, in a yet unpublished paper,[12] challenge the thesis that altruism is thus based on a historically prior egoism, point to implausibilities in the conditioning explanations and suggest intrinsic altruistic motivation from the start, which is innate. But this is not the place to enter into an age-old controversy dating back to Hobbes, Butler and Hume.

Whatever the origin of this response the next important stage comes when the infant is capable of grasping object-permanence, especially that of persons. Empathy or sympathy can then be felt for someone whom the child appreciates as being distinct from himself – usually his mother – although, in Piaget's view the child's outlook is still basically egocentric. The next crucial step is when the child's egocentricism gives way to role-taking and the child begins to realise that others have different points of view. Piaget puts this stage quite late – at 7 to 8 years. But Hoffman argues that in familiar and highly motivating natural settings rudiments of role-taking may begin several years earlier. It culminates in an awareness by the child that others have their own personal identity, their own life circumstances and inner states. (This proceeds with his sense of his own personal identity and distinctiveness.) So the child would continue to react to the momentary distress of others but would feel worse if he knew that it was chronic. With further cognitive development the person may acquire the capacity to comprehend the plight not only of an individual but also of an entire group or class to whom he is exposed – rather like Hume's postulated transition from 'limited benevolence' to 'the sentiment for humanity'. Hoffman produces a certain amount of evidence to support the direct connection between altruistic motivation and action, though he admits that this is more likely when the appropriate thing to do is obvious. He stresses, however, the costs to the observer and the strength of competing motives aroused in him by the situation – especially in an individualistic society.

Hoffman suggests four hypotheses about experiences that may help to foster altruistic motivation:

(i) Allowing the child to have the normal run of distress experiences rather than shielding him from them.
(ii) Providing the child with opportunities for role-taking and for giving help and responsible care to others.
(iii) Encouraging the child to imagine himself in the place of others.
(iv) Exposure for a long time to loved models who behave altruistically.

This is a suggestive, if speculative, story about how we may come to care about others. It suffers, however, from a certain kind of coarseness in that, for instance, the concern felt by a boy for the suffering of one of his gang surely differs qualitatively from that felt by an adolescent for someone whom he knows more intimately as an individual. It may be possible, equally speculatively, to refine this account a bit by making use of some work done by Secord and Peevers[13] on children's perception of others. For emotional responses depend always on a cognitive core, on how the situation is perceived, especially other people in it. More refinement on the cognitive side of Hoffman's theory should have the effect not only of introducing more qualitative distinctions but also of bringing it closer to the Piaget–Kohlberg type of framework. For this was the type of framework that Peevers and Secord used.

They found, for instance, under the aspect of ego-involvement in descriptions of others, that most descriptions used by kindergarten children were saturated with references to the other person's attitude to themselves. Seventh grade children, on the other hand, tended to use descriptions involving mutuality. 'We' or 'us' occurred frequently. The other person was regarded, as it were, as a comrade. At the eleventh grade predominant use is made of other-oriented items. The most dramatic feature of the findings was the growth of the use of other-oriented terms with age, although egocentric and mutual items appear at all ages.

Depth of description was another important developmental dimension. The child starts at level one with simple descriptions locating a person in terms of his possessions, role, social setting, superficial qualities and global characteristics. At level two descriptions are more sophisticated, involving contradictory or amusing characteristics, conditions under which the other person exhibits qualities, references to trying, and so on. At level three *explanations* of characteristics begin to appear. These types of causal-genetic descriptions are rare and do not begin to appear until the high school and college level.

If we transpose these findings about the perception of others to the cognitive aspect of consideration for others, they would suggest that early on sympathetic responses are likely to be tinged with egocentricity. Children would be more likely to respond in this way to those who liked or loved them. This would be followed by the stage of mutuality, Piaget's stage of realism. Others would be regarded as pals; there would be loyalty to comrades. Sympathy for others would not be highly personalised but would be directed towards an individual as a member of the same group. A feeling of fraternity would overlay responses to individuals. At the final level sympathetic reaction to another in distress would be to him as an individual in his own right. Questions of motive and understanding in depth would make the response more discriminating and a degree of objectivity in attitude would supersede the earlier overlays of egocentricity and mutuality. Disinterested care for another human being as a person would be possible, even though it might, at times, be tinged with traces of the earlier attitudes of egocentricity and mutuality.

I appreciate only too well that this account is no more than what Plato called a 'likely story' though it takes the form, not of a myth, but of a report of a limited number of psychological studies. It does have the merit, however, of being more or less consistent with the Piaget–Kohlberg view of cognitive development. As affect does not float about in us unattached but is dependent upon our interpretations of the world and other people, if there is any truth in the Piaget–Kohlberg developmental account, the affective supplement to it must be something like this in rough outline. In a previous publication[14] I actually suggested a very similar account of stages of understanding other people before I had ever read Peevers and Secord!

(2) Negative motivations
The affective aspect of morals covers not only positive motivations such as sympathy and consideration for others: it includes also more

negative ones such as shame and guilt. The most straightforward of these, from Kohlberg's or anyone else's point of view, is shame. For this is the emotion most characteristic of transgressors at what he calls the 'good boy' stage of morality. It is felt by the individual who is conscious that he has let the side down, or not lived up to what is expected of him in the sight of his peers. As Rawls has pointed out[15] there is a close connection between shame and self-respect. One can feel ashamed of one's appearance or slow-wittedness, which is natural shame. Moral shame is occasioned by falling short of virtues that a person's plan of life encourages. The self is diminished and usually other people, who draw attention to such shortcomings, are the main agents of this feeling of self-diminishment. Kohlberg actually makes no mention of shame in his chart of 'motives for engaging in moral action'.[16] But he could easily have included it in stage three or four.

Guilt is much more difficult to deal with because of the voluminous writings about it by the Freudian school, set in motion by the concept of the super-ego. But whether an account is given in terms of identification and introjection, or whether a social learning theory such as that of Aronfreed[17] is adopted, it seems undeniable that quite early on children internalise rules, the breaking of which occasions a feeling of guilt. This is often called 'authority guilt', because the prohibitions, on account of their source, are likely to be tinged with other natural emotions such as fear and anxiety, on account of the possibility of punishment or of the withdrawal of love. Presumably, in Piagetian terms, it begins to manifest itself when the child is passing to the stage of moral realism, when he sees rules, as Durkheim put it, *comme les choses*, and not just egocentrically.

This, however, is only one type of guilt which may be prevalent in certain types of societies. In the psychoanalytic literature another type of guilt has been postulated. Money-Kyrle,[18] for instance, who owed much to Melanie Klein, claimed that Freud's theory was one-sided because it dealt only with the authoritarian conscience. There is also the humanistic conscience which has its origin in the 'guilt' experienced in hating and hurting the mother, the first object of the child's love. In its earliest form it would surely be somewhat imprecise to call this 'guilt', as 'guilt' presupposes acting contrary to one's sense of right and justice. And infants can scarcely be credited with such concepts. Nevertheless, if there is anything in such hypothesis – and who can cross their heart and say honestly that they understand what is meant to be going on when they read the writings of Klein, Fairbairn, Guntrip, *et al.* – it would provide a fitting negative parallel to the Hoffman hypothesis about the origins of altruism. The point is that in guilt we tend to focus on the infringement of claims of others and on injuries done to them, whereas in shame we are more sensitive to our own loss of self-esteem and our disappointment in being unable to live up to our ideals. So though there is authority guilt in which doing wrong is associated with anxiety and fear of punishment from parents or parent-substitutes, there must also be some origin to straightforward guilt which is not so associated, and which is what we feel when we injure others or infringe some accepted rule such as that of honesty or promise-keeping. Whether we feel guilt or shame when we fail to live up to Kohlberg's principle of justice depends on how self-referentially we view it. We may even feel remorse which seems to be a mixture of guilt at wrongdoing and shame that we could be the sort of person to do such a wrong.

THE CONTENT OF MORALITY

So much for speculations about the affective side of moral development which I have tried to make consistent with Kohlberg's cognitive theory. I pass now to a few observations about the content of morality which is the other glaring omission in Kohlberg's scheme. This omission is not one of inadvertence; for he repeatedly says that a 'bag of virtues' is unimportant in a person's moral equipment. It must first be remarked that he has quite a bag himself at stages five and six which make them quite unlike earlier stages where rules are linked to general attitudes such as approval of authority figures and peers, reward and punishment. When he comes to the principled stage of morality, justice, human welfare, respect for persons and society appear as principles. But why just these? A principle is merely a consideration to which we appeal in order to justify a rule or practice. Promise-keeping would be functioning as a principle, for instance, if it was used to justify a person's refusal to entertain divorce. Presumably Kohlberg has in mind those principles which are fundamental to the use of reason, for which it is difficult to argue that further reasons can be given. Why not then include truth-telling? For Peter Winch[19] has argued that this principle is a presupposition of human communication. This may be too strong a thesis actually; but a good case can be made out for it as a presupposition of the descriptive, explanatory and argumentative uses of language, which would include moral reasoning. At the principled level of morality Kohlberg would then have quite a formidable bag of virtues – justice, benevolence, respect and truth-telling.

But what of his claims for the unimportance of lower-level content which can be justified by appeal to such principles? Well, the first and obvious points to make are logical ones:

(a) It is very important that children should firmly internalise a set of rules so that they know what it is to act on a rule in a non-egocentric fashion. Unless they do this they have not the necessary basis to reflect on rules in the light of principles and to accept or reject those which they deem justifiable or non-justifiable.

(b) Content vitally affects the application of principles both in the lives of societies and individuals. What counts as welfare, for instance, depends very much on current social practices and individual needs (a normative notion). The application of justice depends on whether need is thought more important than desert. And so on. There is no slide-rule for applying abstract principles to concrete situations. How they are applied, which is often highly controversial, depends upon judgement and what Kohlberg calls the 'content' of morality in a given society. And unless there were a determinate content principles would have no function; for they are what we appeal to when we criticise or justify some lower-level form of conduct.

I pass now to more practical considerations that concern us as parents, teachers and citizens. Thomas Hobbes once made the sobering remark that even a small child can kill a grown man while he is asleep. His fearful imagination conjures up a picture of a home in which the children set fire to the curtains, break all the windows and torture the cat. Why is not such exuberance more common? For the parents cannot be ever-present supervisors. Presumably because the children have internalised a set of rules which inhibit them from doing certain things. The same applies to schools, though in certain areas teachers have an uphill task in getting children to observe a reasonable code of conduct. We are in the same boat as citizens; for given that every underground and dark alley cannot be patrolled by the police and given that, on Kohlberg's figures, only a very small minority of the population reach his stage of principled morality, it is absolutely essential that the vast majority get well bedded down in a basic code at stages three and four. For if you are assaulted and have your wallet taken it is the content of the assailant's code that matters to you, not speculations about whether he has passed from stage one to two.

The point is that there are certain basic rules of content, in addition to Kohlberg's principles, such as keeping your contracts, preserving property whether public or private, not stealing, the general observance of which is essential to the maintenance of social life under almost any conceivable conditions. These can be straightforwardly justified by an appeal to Kohlberg's principles and are in a different category from controversial rules like those relating to sexual practices and trade unions. It is absolutely essential that in this area of basic rules there should be a high degree of conformity, whether people conform on principled grounds or whether their conformity is of the conventional type. We cannot rely just on the law.

Kohlberg admits that, though progression from stage to stage cannot be directly taught, content can be. And so we return full circle to the picture presented at the start by Skinner and his advocacy of systematic teaching of basic social virtues backed up by positive reinforcement. Now I am not a Skinnerian. Indeed I have been very critical all my academic life, not just of Skinner,[20] but of behaviourism generally as a movement in psychology.[21] But I do see virtue in the systematic holding-up of standards to young children, backed up by approval. I do see virtue in the modelling advocated by social learning theorists and the kind of atmosphere in the home and infant school which permits the use of what Hoffman[22] calls 'induction', which is a kind of elementary moral instruction. Maybe, as Hoffman claims, some mild forms of power assertion are necessary as well to draw attention to what is important. But it should not be severe so that learning is constantly inhibited by fear and anxiety. I see virtue in these sorts of techniques not just because of the evidence produced by Hoffman and others but because, if Piaget and Kohlberg are right about the early stages of morality, there is no other way that a rule is meaningful to a small child as a guide to conduct except as linked with approval and disapproval, reward and punishment. There would be no point in general in having such rules, unless they regulated wayward inclinations, so conformity usually demands the presence of some counter-inclination such as the desire for approval or reward, as at this age the child cannot see their point deriving from principles.

At the same time, of course, there will be encouragement of the sense of justice and concern for others that are *later* to serve as principles if the child gets to the principled stage. The problem of moral education, from this view, is how to encourage these embryonic principles and how to teach a basic content so that Kohlberg's progression will take place. Some techniques, which we call indoctrination, fixate a person at his 'good boy' stage and positively discourage him from passing to a stage at which the content which has been absorbed will be reflected upon critically in the light of principles. And are those people, popularised by the Freudian school, who become fixated at an early stage with extreme feelings of guilt and unworthiness about their conduct, victims of punitive and rejecting parental techniques of child-rearing? Development is equally likely to be stunted by permissiveness, whether this involves indeterminacy in relation to what is expected or no determinate expectations; for the anxiety created by such conditions of inconsistency or anomie are not conducive to learning. Also there is little predictability in such an environment which is essential for learning to grasp the consequences of actions, and the child gets little feed-back from parents, which he interprets as indifference. I would hazard the guess that self-respect, which is later connected with shame, is one of the most important factors in moral character. On some views it is closely connected with will or ego-strength, the importance of which Kohlberg admits. But self-respect depends enormously on the messages about them which children read off from ways in which they are treated; it is not just, as Freudians have argued, a matter of internalising the qualities of admired adults.

It may well be that this content, is, to a certain extent, situation-specific. But so are high-order principles such as justice, the consideration of others and truth-telling, in that differing social contexts as well as judgement are involved in their application. It may be that there is much inconsistency and back-sliding in following a code of conduct that constitutes the content of morality. But the degree of this will depend upon the degree of continuity in the presence of reinforcers such as approval. The same applies to a principled morality if it is not backed up by strength of will, which can also help, as Kohlberg admits, at the level of content.

Of course the stage of conventional morality has its defects. I am not arguing for its moral superiority – only for its logical necessity and practical necessity in any account of the moral life. I am insisting that more thought needs to be given to its content and to the methods by which it is taught. For given that small children cannot see the rationale for it in terms of principles, and given that, for the reasons which I have outlined, they have to learn such a basic code, the problem is to employ methods of teaching it to them which are effective without being indoctrinatory, and which prepare the way for a principled morality later. If parents and teachers withdraw too much and refrain from acting as models we are likely to get the sort of phenomena described by Bronfenbrenner in his chapter on 'The unmaking of the American child'.[23] If they are too authoritarian and punitive we are likely to get individuals who are indoctrinated or crippled with irrational guilt. What we want to know is the middle road that is likely to lead to Kohlberg's heroes such as Martin Luther King.

REFERENCES: CHAPTER 7

1 Bronfenbrenner, U., *Two Worlds of Childhood* (London: Allen & Unwin, 1971), chs 1, 2.
2 Kohlberg, L., 'Moral education in the schools', *School Review*, no. 74 (1966), pp. 1–30.
3 Kohlberg, L., 'Development of moral character and ideology', in Hoffman, M.L. (ed.), *Review of Child Development Research*, Vol. 1 (New York: Russell Sage Foundation, 1964).
4 Peters, R.S. 'Moral development: a plea for pluralism', in Peters, R.S., *Psychology and Ethical Development*, (London: Allen & Unwin, 1974).
5 Kurtines, W., and Greif, E.B., 'The development of moral thought: review and evaluation of Kohlberg's approach', *Psychology Bulletin*, vol. 81, no. 8 (August 1974).
6 Gibbs, J.C., 'Kohlberg's stages of moral judgement: a constructive critique', *Harvard Educational Review.*, vol. 47, no. 1 (February 1977).

7 Garbarino, J., and Bronfenbrenner, U., 'The socialization of moral judgment and behaviour in cross-cultural perspective', in Lickona, T. (ed.), *Moral Development and Behaviour* (New York: Holt, Rinehart & Winston, 1976).

8 Turiel, E., 'An experimental test of the sequentiality of development stages in the child's moral judgements', *Journal of Personality and Social Psychology*, vol. 3 (1966), pp. 611–18.
Turiel, E., 'Developmental processes in the child's moral thinking', in Mussen, P.H., Langer, J., and Covington, M. (eds), *Trends and Issues in Developmental Psychology* (New York: Holt, Rinehart & Winston, 1969).
Rest, J., 'Patterns of preference and comprehension in moral judgements', *Journal of Personality*, vol. 41 (1973), pp. 86–109.

9 Peters, R.S., 'The development of reason', in Peters, R.S., *Psychology and Ethical Development* (London: Allen & Unwin, 1974).

10 McPhail, P., Ungoed-Thomas, J.R., and Chapman, H., *Moral Education in the Secondary School* (London: Longman, 1972).

11 Hoffman, M.L. 'Empathy, role-taking, guilt and development of altruistic motives', in Lickona, T. (ed.), *Moral Development and Behaviour* (New York: Holt, Rinehart & Winston, 1976).

12 Sebastian, I., and Wren, T., 'The origin of the altruistic response', unpublished.

13 Secord, P.F., and Peevers, B.H., 'The development of person concepts', in Mischel, T. (ed.), *Understanding Other Persons* (Oxford: Blackwell, 1974).

14 Peters, R.S., 'Personal understanding and personal relationships', in Mischel, T. (ed.), *Understanding Other Persons* (Oxford: Blackwell, 1974)

15 Rawls, J., *A Theory of Justice* (Cambridge, Mass.: Harvard University Press, 1971), p. 444.

16 Kohlberg, L., 'From is to ought', in Mischel, T. (ed.), *Cognitive Development and Epistemology* (New York: Academic Press, 1971).

17 Aronfreed, J., 'Moral development from the standpoint of a general psychological theory', in Lickona, T. (ed.), *Moral Development and Moral Behaviour* (New York: Holt, Rinehart & Winston, 1976), p. 170.

18 Money-Kyrle, R., *Psycho-analysis and Politics* (London: Duckworth, 1951).

19 Winch, P. 'Nature and convention', *Proceedings of the Aristotelian Society*, 1959–60; reprinted in Winch, P., *Ethics and Action* (London: Routledge & Kegan Paul, 1972).

20 See 'Survival or the soul' in Peters, R.S., *Psychology and Ethical Development* (London: Allen & Unwin, 1974).

21 See op. cit., chs 1 and 2, and Peters, R.S., *The Concept of Motivation* (London: Routledge & Kegan Paul, 1958).

22 See Hoffman, M.L., 'Moral development', in Mussen, P.A. (ed.), *Carmichael's Manual of Child Psychology*, Vol. 2 (New York: Wiley, 1970), *passim*.

23 See Bronfenbrenner, U., *Two Worlds of Childhood* (London: Allen & Unwin, 1971).

Chapter 8

Motivation and Education*

AN INTRODUCTORY PICTURE

As educators I think most of us have some ideal of learning. We would wish to see children learning either because they just enjoy learning or because what they learn is of significance to them in their lives. By this I do not just mean that a girl should devote herself attentively to biology, for instance, because she wants to be a doctor. I mean also that she might find herself absorbed, say, in reading George Eliot because the issues are of emotional significance to her. In such cases the task of learning exerts its own discipline over time because of the interest or significance to the learner of its content. There is no need for goading or bribing by others, especially by teachers.

In schools, however, this ideal of learning is only patchily realised. More often, if children do apply themselves to learning, it is because of some kind of extrinsic motivation. By that I mean some kind of further end influences them which has no close connection with the content of what has to be learnt. They may learn either biology or literature to avoid punishment, to pass an examination, or to please a teacher. But the content of what they are learning may be of no interest or signifi- cance to them. What matters is the pay off. This kind of motivation may be effective in a society like ours in which the question 'where does that get you?' or 'what is the pay off?' is so frequently asked. But it is counter-productive in that it leads just to mugging up things that are soon forgotten and in that it encourages an undesirable attitude towards learning. And does the learning last?

Another form of motivation, which seems to be more often exemp- lified at the primary level, is intrinsic motivation. By this I mean learning situations when the inducements to learn are intrinsic to what

* This essay is an abbreviated and revised version of a symposium of which I, represent- ing philosophy, was chairman, and in which R. Colquhoun, a sociologist, and Mrs C.M. Killick, a psychologist (both from Goldsmith's College, University of London), also participated, though they had no hand in the abbreviation and rewriting. It is meant to be an attempt at approaching educational theory in the manner suggested in my article 'Den teoretiske paedagogiks uregerlighed', *Paedagogik*, vol. 7, no. 3 (1977) (Gjel- lerup) ('The intractability of educational theory'). My thanks are due to them for their contributions which I hope that I have not too much distorted.

is being learnt. A child may just find something very puzzling and want an explanation; he may wish to master some task that is challenging; he may attend to something because it catches his interest. This type of motivation is obviously one of the types that conforms to the educator's ideal. But there are problems about it in schools. Some children seem to come much more strongly influenced by it than others. There is the problem of sustaining this kind of motivation when learning tasks become difficult. Also it seems to be much more apparent at the primary than at the secondary level of education. Maybe our schools do a lot of discourage it!

Finally there are various social aspects of motivation that are not easy to classify as either extrinsic or intrinsic because their manner of operation is not very well understood. Obviously, for instance, the example of others, of older children or of teachers, who exhibit various skills and abilities and who adopt certain attitudes towards potential learners, is influential. So too is the general institutional framework in which the child has to learn; for this incorporates determinate expectations of the learners. Its size as well as its social climate will probably make a difference to the motivation to learn.

(1) EXTRINSIC MOTIVATION

Let us now have a more detailed look at these types of theories.

(a) Sociological

Most sociologists would agree that at least since the beginning of industrialisation important areas of social life in Western societies have been organised on instrumental principles, in particular those of production and consumption. It also seems to be the case that in work and other contexts many people do act in terms of such 'extrinsic' motives as the pursuit of wealth, prestige and power. Much of the sociological debate about such issues has centred on Marx's concept of 'alienation'. By 'alienation' Marx meant:

First the fact that labour is *external* to the worker, that is, it does not belong to his essential being; that in his work therefore he does not affirm himself, does not feel content but unhappy, does not develop in his physical and mental energy but mortifies his body and ruins his mind. The worker therefore only feels himself outside his work, and in his work feels outside himself. He is at home when he is not working, and when he is working he is not at home. His labour is therefore not voluntary but coerced: it is forced labour. It is therefore not the satisfaction of a need; it is merely a means to satisfy needs external to it. Its alien character emerges clearly in . . . that as soon as no physical or other compulsion exists, labour is shunned like the plague.[1]

Such a description may be applicable, as a number of writers[2] are now arguing, to the pupils who at best do no more than put up with school and leave as soon as they are legally able; but it may also be of relevance to pupils working for 'good results' – such as some of the 'successful' working-class grammar school boys – as well as a valid description of how some teachers experience their work.[3]

It is a commonplace, too, that in 'advanced' industrial societies there is an ever-expanding 'need' for professional, scientific and technologically expert manpower, and that social status and mobility have come to be increasingly dependent on formal educational qualifications.[4] It is said, in other words, that there is a 'close link' between 'the educational system', 'the economy' and 'the occupational structure', which encourages an extrinsic type of motivation. The implication seems to be that this 'close link' between schooling, social mobility and occupation must somehow be weakened if teachers are to be allowed to get on with their work of *education* under less constraint from the 'extrinsic demands of the economy'.

(b) Psychological

Psychologists, of course, have much to say about extrinsic motivation.

(i) Drive-reduction.

The theory of drives or need-reduction, which dominated psychology for about thirty years, was of this sort. It was based on W. B. Cannon's physiological theory of homeostasis, which showed how various mechanisms in the body operate to restore a state of equilibrium, when there is a departure from it in, for instance, a hunger state.[5] Deficit states, such as those of hunger, were called by psychologists states of need, and the hypothesis was that all behaviour is originally motivated by the overall tendency to restore a steady state of equilibrium. In the course of development subsidiary or secondary needs or drives are alleged to be formed, in the first place because the obtaining of the particular goal is associated with reduction of some basic need. It was assumed by Clark Hull[6] and others that any behaviour that tends to restore homeostatic balance and thus to reduce tension is stamped in, strengthened and learnt.

This theory was developed by Hull for the explanation of behaviour generally.[7] He was not particularly concerned with classroom learning. Most of the work was done on biological needs such as hunger, thirst and sex, which have marginal application to the classroom; for we would scarcely contemplate putting children into these need-states in order to provide some motivation for them to learn. As the theory of secondary drives or needs was always highly speculative,[8] the relevance to education of this classic work on extrinsic motivation was always dubious. Hence the plight of generations of psychology teachers who delved into their textbooks to extract some findings that might throw some light on why children did not want to learn!

(*ii*) *Skinner*. Of much more relevance to the classroom, however, has been the work of B.F. Skinner who put forward a much more popular theory of extrinsic motivation. In his theory of operant conditioning he laid great stress on positive reinforcement. His assumption is that responses are made more probable or more frequent if they are initially reinforced. He believes that all human behaviour is, or can be, a product of operant conditioning, and this includes learning in the classroom.[9]

What are we to make of such theories? Let us leave on one side the classic drive theory of people like Hull; for, there is little mileage in the use of basic biological needs such as hunger and thirst in the classroom. The weight must be borne by secondary needs, such as the need for approval, whose status in the classic theory is a bit dubious. So we might as well concentrate on Skinner's theory in which use is made of positive reinforcers such as approval and reward. For his theory is the most relevant to the classroom of all theories of extrinsic motivation. But there is a problem about it; for what does Skinner do about obvious cases covered by theories of intrinsic motivation in which children are encouraged to go on learning because they get things right? Are there not a multitude of cases like this which are difficult to fit into his theory?

Actually Skinner and his followers are only too well aware of such cases and have built an explanation of them into their theory. Zigler and Kanzer,[10] for instance, argue that there is what they call a 'developmentally changing reinforcer hierarchy'. That is, early in learning, children need to be dependent upon some extrinsic tangible reward. This dependence diminishes as social reinforcements, such as affection, praise and attention, become increasingly effective. At a still later stage these become the cue for the administration of self-reinforcement. They assert that children gradually become more concerned about being right for being right's sake. No doubt this development often occurs, though it still leaves open the possibility of learning out of curiosity, for instance, which proceeds without such social reinforcement. But it illustrates one of the problems that philosophers have with a psychologist such as Skinner who is so cavalier with his concepts. The concept of 'reinforcement' was originally used to pick out cases in which some kind of act, such as pressing a bar, is associated with some other disconnected stimulus, such as a pellet of food. This is named a positive reinforcement because it helps learning. Reinforcers in the first place are extrinsic to learning, things like pellets of food, smiles, and so on. It is then found that children sometimes learn things without such extrinsic aids. As we say, they do things out of curiosity, or because they like getting things right. These cases were actually, historically speaking, produced as *refutations* of the theory of reinforcement as an all-inclusive explanatory theory of learning. But the theorist, instead of admitting the limitations of his theory, includes the counter-example in the theory by extending the range of the original concept. In this case, for instance, he says that in such cases children are reinforcing themselves instead of saying that some other sort of explanation is required. Thus, as Chomsky showed in his celebrated review of Skinner's *Verbal Behaviour*,[11] the concept of 'reinforcement' becomes so general that it no longer does any work.

Skinner himself, however, is totally uninterested in such criticisms of his theory of operant conditioning. He has always maintained, with whatever plausibility, that he avoids theory and just sticks to empirical data provided by the careful observation of organisms. His, he claims, is a strictly operational-engineering type of approach. He is interested in control rather than explanation. He wants to build human beings rather like an engineer builds a bridge; for him behaviour is something to manipulate rather than to explain. Adopting, therefore, this pragmatic type of approach he sees learning as nothing but a change in the probability of response. He finds that this probability changes if changes are made in the contingencies of reinforcement or factors affecting the probability of response. This terminology does not confuse him in getting on with the job of shaping behaviour and this is what matters. He repeatedly states how inefficient teachers are in the classroom, both in the ways in which they present the content to be learned and in the random way in which they reinforce children. More attention to properly sequenced learning, such as can be provided by teaching machines, and to schedules of reinforcement is likely to prove much more beneficial in practice than arguing about the precise meaning of words.

Now this is all very well. But the type of language which he uses, and which he extends to cover situations quite inappropriate to it, is part and parcel of Skinner's whole system of thought and of his approach to human beings and human problems. His lack of interest in the nature of what he calls 'reinforcing events', his disregard for what goes on inside people, especially their inner life of thought and feeling, is symptomatic of his instrumental manipulative approach. In his book *Beyond Freedom and Dignity*[12] he explicitly states that the great enemy of his manipulative paternalistic approach to human problems is the pathetic belief of human beings in their own freedom and dignity. Philosophers nowadays are often attacked by sociologists with only a smattering of philosophical understanding for the attention which they pay to concepts. But any philosopher worth his salt is only interested in concepts for the light which they shed on people's assumptions, presuppositions, valuations, and so on. They provide a convenient way into criticising and discussing what lies behind them. Skinner's conceptual apparatus is symptomatic of a general approach to human life. Pointing out the way in which he extends certain types of concepts is only a preliminary to mounting an attack on his whole conception of human life and of how change ought to be brought about. His theory of motivation, especially his view of the importance in life of what he calls 'reinforcement', sheds light on the sort of creature that he thinks that man is.

The trouble with this kind of model is that it misses a fundamentally important characteristic of man which distinguishes him from both the objects of the physical world studied by the scientist and from the rats, pigeons and other animals studied by the experimental psychologist: I mean, of course, the fact that man does not just mindlessly respond to the stimuli, pressures and events of his environment. He has *consciousness*. He interprets the situations in which he finds himself in his everyday life; he gives those situations meaning; and he is acting on his world, rather than merely reacting to it.

Another major problem with behaviourist accounts of learning is that they appear to see the individual as always learning on his own. In a sense this is, of course, true: others cannot learn for us. But my point is that, unlike the animals in the psychologist's artificially contrived and 'controlled' experiments, human beings in the situations of everyday lives are members of social worlds. It may often be that we ignore the fact that man is born into a social world mapped out and interpreted for him by others – parents, other relations, friends, teachers, and so on. Now in this sense it is rather as though man is in a situation controlled by others, rather like the animal in the situation controlled by the experimental psychologist. So, seemingly, man is confined and limited in his social world and its meaning is made *for* him. But, at the same time, he, as a *human* being, interprets that world, even though others interpret it for him. He makes his own nuances of meaning and may act in spite of, and not just because of, the standard social meanings and circumstances which are said to condition him. The danger for teachers in adopting a Skinnerian viewpoint on the teaching-learning situation is that they may come to think of, and act towards, pupils as 'empty vessels' to be filled up with the teacher's knowledge, rather than conceive of pupils as active agents in the learning process.

(*iii*) *The needs of the child*. Another extrinsic model is put forward by progressives who argue that learning should be based on the needs of the child. Now I do not want to deny the importance of needs like those of approval or security as motivational aids to learning. But more is meant than this by the progressives; they think that the content of learning should be determined by children's needs.

This more ambitious claim surely needs examination, which must begin with the concept of 'need'. Reference to 'needs' implies a lack of something that is necessary for some state thought desirable. Thus we speak of a need for food when we think of the absence of food in relation to some state, like that of survival, which we assume to be desirable. This is a case of a biological need. There are other needs, of a psychological sort, like those for love and security, which pick out conditions necessary for some state of minimal functioning, often called 'mental health', which is thought of as a *sine qua non* of any tolerable type of human life. Then there are other needs which are obviously related to some approved pattern of life in society. We might talk, for instance, of the need to be independent.

Now if we are thinking of what children should learn at school, which constitutes a curriculum, my case is that the appeal to 'needs', which is meant to give scientific respectability to the child-centred approach, is not very helpful. For the needs which have been shown to be motivating in terms of such theories are largely irrelevant in determining the content of what should be learnt at school. Hunger, thirst and love do not suggest goals to which we would contemplate harnessing a lot of school learning. On the other hand needs relating to socially approved ways of behaving such as cleanliness or independence do provide such goals. We might say that a boy needs a bath or that our children need independence. The trouble, however, with these goals is that they are not motivating. If they were we would have little problem with moral education! In the context, therefore, of determining the curriculum, the appeal to 'needs' functions mainly as a way of stating socially approved goals and standards from the child's point of view. But these aims are not necessarily very motivating.

We can, however, think of 'needs' as providing aids to learning the content of which we have decided on other grounds. I doubt if anyone would contemplate starving a child to provide an incentive for him to learn to read or do some mathematics. But many people see nothing wrong in harnessing his need for approval in the service of such learning. Similarly most teachers nowadays would be chary of teaching in such a way that children felt rejected or unloved. So what are often called psychological needs do seem relevant to learning, at least as aids to it. Indeed, looking at the situation in schools realistically, it is

motivation in the case of some of the children whom we have to teach. My objection to people like Skinner is that they go too far in this direction, not that they have not highlighted a form of motivation that is very important in teaching. The hope is that, if children do start off by being purely extrinsically motivated, some other form of motivation, of a more intrinsic sort, will gradually take over, exemplifying Allport's principle of 'functional autonomy'.[13] Or motivation may be mixed.

As a matter of fact educationalists, especially those of child-centred persuasions, often refer to intrinsic motivation in terms of 'needs'. They talk, for instance, of the need for novelty or for stimulation, which is part of the intrinsic motivation package. Perhaps, then, we had better pass to intrinsic motivation and see what sorts of inducements to learn are included in it.

(2) INTRINSIC MOTIVATION

Intrinsic motivation has been most in evidence at the primary level of schooling. Historically speaking the most influential doctrine, which has some relationship to psychology, is that which has emphasised the importance of play. But it is necessary to make a distinction at this point; for some have argued that learning should be *like* play, whereas others have argued the much stronger thesis that children learn a lot when they are literally playing.

(a) Play

The first doctrine, that learning should be like play, has a long and tenacious history. It goes back at least as far as Plato who declared that enforced learning will not stay in the mind. So compulsion ought to be avoided and children's lessons should take the form of play. Down the centuries different aspects of play have been picked out as support for this belief. It has been noted, for instance, that when children are playing they are interested and hence absorbed in what they are doing; their attention-span is considerable. So, it has been argued, children's learning should be related to their interests; for in this way their attention will be caught, and attention is crucial to learning. Others stress that play is essentially pleasurable, something done for its own sake. So if things can be found to which children adopt a similar stance, this will enhance their learning.

Some have therefore argued that teachers should disguise what has to be learned and present it to children in the form of toys. Learning from such toys should therefore become like play for children. In the early part of this century, too, Caldwell Cook advocated his special 'play-way' in education.[14] He argued that without interest there is no learning. One of the main features of play is the interest which children show in their activities. Therefore learning should take the form of play. He worked out quite an elaborate method to show teachers how to contrive such learning by trying to tap children's interests.

The second, and stronger, doctrine maintains that play is of crucial importance in education because children learn all sorts of things of educational importance while they are playing. The main trouble, however, is that there is little agreement amongst theorists of play about what its function is in relation to learning.[15] Karl Groos, for instance, saw play as the product of emerging instincts. It fixes them and exercises them in preparation for their time of maturation in life proper. So in their play children are rehearsing their adult roles in life. Stanley Hall, on the other hand, assumed that play is not an activity that develops skills which will be useful in the service of developing instinctive patterns of behaviour. Rather it serves to rid the individual of unnecessary instinctual skills that are relics of an earlier stage in the evolution of man. He postulated that each child passes through a series of play stages, corresponding to and recapitulating the cultural stages of the race. Caldwell Cook used this theory to support his emphasis on play. Freud thought that in play the child is gratifying the instinctual demands of the id for instant gratification. It is difficult to conjecture what the child might be learning on this theory. For Erikson, on the other hand, play is characterised by mastery. He modified Freud's view of it by stressing that children are driven to play by their wish to take an active role in painful encounters that have been passively experienced. So in playing the child is learning to master conflicts.

Last there is Piaget's theory of play. For him play represents just an immature form of thinking. It consists in bending reality to fit one's form of thought, in assimilation for assimilation's sake.[16] Children are thus not really learning anything; they are just strengthening existing mental structures which are necessary for later logical thinking.

From a psychologist's point of view it is distressing that, while so much importance is attached to play by educators, there is so little evidence about what children actually learn while they are playing. Most of the assertions made by theorists about the function of play are sheer speculation. There are also many different forms of play, and different forms may have a different function.[17] It would indeed be helpful to have some solid evidence about this. About thirty years ago I used to run a youth centre on premises which we shared with a nursery school. The teacher there was extremely keen on children playing with sand and water. I asked why this was so important. Her view was that it helped children to deal with their emotional conflicts in some way. Twenty years later I visited a lot of primary schools and there again was the old sand and water. I asked what this did for the children. I was told by the teacher that playing with it was of crucial importance in assisting their conceptual development. It is as if teachers are well aware that children love to play and find different educational reasons for encouraging them to do what they enjoy doing. And, of course, there is no reason to suppose that, if they are learning anything, they are learning the same sort of thing when they are playing with sand and water, when they are playing shops and when they are playing at mothers and fathers.

But play is only one type of intrinsic motivation. There are others who have singled out other ways of viewing learning which are claimed to be motivating – for example, curiosity, the need for achievement, competence, and so on. These are more precise theories than the appeal to play.

(b) Berlyne and Piaget

Berlyne, for instance, has tried, with difficulty, to remain with the old drive theorists like Hull, whilst at the same time stressing the importance of curiosity or 'epistemic drive'. He claims that there are properties within the environment, such as novelty, complexity, ambiguity and incongruity, which arouse the child's curiosity. What these have in common is that they give rise to cognitive conflict. But it has to be an optimal amount of these properties. Too much is rejected or ignored; too little occasions boredom.[18] He suggested that this kind of motivation, if skilfully employed by teachers, will increase the retention of new material as well as improve the understanding of it. It will occasion the active search for information and problem-solving by directed thinking.[19] Berlyne's theory is very similar to Piaget's, although Piaget is very antipathetic to the stimulus–response type of heritage from which Berlyne's theory developed. Piaget believes that 'disequilibrium' or conflict arises from a lack of match between properties of the environment and the child's conceptual scheme, which is exhibited in discrepancies and inconsistencies in the environment. The striving towards 'equilibration' pushes the child towards more logical ways of thinking and is the driving force of cognitive development.[20]

This shows both the strength and weakness of Piaget's theory and of many psychological theories like his which make what is being asserted sound much more 'scientific' than it in fact is. Surely what Piaget is saying is that consistency is crucial to our understanding of rational thought. We must, therefore, postulate in children, who are developing more rational ways of thinking, some kind of striving for consistency. But nothing more is added of an explanatory sort by wrapping this up in a pseudo-scientific model by talk of 'equilibration'. This has not the explanatory value of the similar postulate of homeostasis in Cannon's *Wisdom of the Body*. For, as I have argued elsewhere,[21] homeostasis does work as an explanation at the bodily level because it is possible to specify the deficit states that initiate the behaviour and the mechanisms by means of which equilibrium is restored in ways independent of the behaviour to be explained. But this is not the case in Piaget's theory. The individual is prompted to assimilate or to accommodate by becoming aware of momentary inconsistencies and discrepancies between what he expects and the situations encountered. But these states of disequilibrium can only be identified by these types of negative relationship to the content of the individual's expectations. There are no independent ways of identifying them. So the tendency towards equilibrium is just a pseudo-scientific description for the behaviour to be explained which can be described in more straight-forward ways. Human beings have a tendency to rid their thinking of inconsistencies, incongruities, contradictions, and so on. They have; and this is very important for our understanding of rationality. But nothing is added to this understanding by introducing the model of 'equilibration'.[22] Nevertheless, Piaget and his followers are on to some points of considerable importance to teachers. For he is not particularly concerned with making learning interesting; his concern is that children should understand what they learn. His message seems to be that teachers should pay less attention to trying to stuff a lot of content into children's minds but should pay more attention to the ways in which their forms of understanding develop. For, in his view, lack of interest is largely the product of lack of understanding, of presenting material to children which is unrelated to their level of mental operating. One of his followers, Hans Furth, has devised all sorts of 'thinking games' which, he claims, do much for improving children's powers to understand.[23]

(c) Achievement motivation

Perhaps more promising, as a form of intrinsic motivation, is McClelland's 'achievement motivation',[24] which he defines as 'competing against a standard of excellence'. This type of motivation, in his view, manifests itself early in childhood and is built on the universal experiences of mastery such as learning to talk, read, write, and so on. All these tasks have their own standards of excellence. There is some later work on the development of achievement by J. Veroff[25] in which it is suggested that this motive of competing against standards of excellence develops out of two earlier forms, which he calls 'autonomous motives' and 'social comparison'. By 'autonomous motives' he means something like White's competence or mastery[26] which occurs in the early years. This gives way in childhood to social comparison which involves competing against peers. Such competition allows the child to learn his own abilities and to learn also about the standards involved in the tasks. After successful completion of this stage the adolescent can then attain true achievement, which is competing against a standard of excellence. But if the former stage has not been completed successfully, then development is, as it were, arrested, and the child remains interested only in doing better than others.

Naturally enough, though the concept is psychological in origin, sociologists quickly took it up, claiming that achievement motivation, taken with 'achievement values', forms an 'achievement syndrome'.[27] Briefly the argument put forward is this. In industrialised societies such as the USA and Britain there exists a dominant value-orientation towards 'achievement'. People in these societies are high in achievement motivation, of which a particular exemplification is the motivation to succeed at school. But it is argued that achievement values and motivation are not present in all social groups to the same degree; for example, the middle class are said to value achievement more highly – witness their job aspirations – and are higher on achievement motivation than the working class; and it is claimed that this 'explains' the apparently well documented social-class differences in educational achievement. Finally, in an attempt to explain how these social-class differences arise, researchers have tried to investigate the effects of child-rearing practices on the development of children's values and motivation to succeed at school.

(3) SOCIAL ASPECTS OF MOTIVATION

I am not sure how firm the evidence is for some of such generalisations suggested by sociologists but certainly I find the general approach congenial. Historically speaking, there has been rather a tendency for psychologists to speak of motivation as if it consisted in inner urges, such as instincts and drives, that propelled human beings towards goals as if they were mechanical systems. Philosophers have been very resistant to this approach to motivation in recent times. Indeed they seem very much to have pioneered the sort of approach that is now being taken up by some sociologists.[28]

(a) Philosophical sketch of motivation

Philosophers argue, mainly against behaviourists in psychology, that no convincing account or explanation of human action can be given unless the agent's view of his situation is made central. Without taking account of this we would not be able to identify the action of a man waving his hand as saying goodbye to a friend, cooling himself, signalling, and so on. When we speak of his 'motives' we have in mind some view which he has of a situation in relation to which the action in question is seen as relevant. For instance, if a man is acting out of jealousy rather than out of anger or fear, he must see the situation as one in which he thinks that someone else has something or is trying to obtain something to which he thinks he has some claim himself. Similarly a man acting out of envy sees someone as having something which he himself wants. In both cases the actions done out of these motives are seen as relevant ways of influencing the situation in relation to his way of viewing it. Of course these ways of viewing situations are affectively tinged. The agent may have inner feelings which go with his way of interpreting the situation. But these are inseparable from the cognitive core of the motive. So instead of thinking of motives as inner causes which push the individual, the philosopher stresses their connection with certain kinds of thoughts. The agent is sensitive to certain considerations about the situation which matter to him. His actions only make sense if account is taken of his prior view of the situation.

Once an active interpreting agent has been made central in an account of motivation then the phenomena must be looked at afresh. How people behave is not just a matter of what they are driven to do by inner mechanisms; it is a matter of how they interpret other people's attitudes to them, what they make of a whole variety of social situations, including institutional contexts such as a school. So if we are considering the motivation of the child at school we must not think of the child entering it with his own private package of drives, interests, and the like. We must consider how the school looks to him, the messages, for instance, which he reads off from its control system and examination structure. We must take account of his understanding of what teachers expect of him, of the view which they take of him in their classifications, and so on. His 'motives' may not be givens which are part of his mental make-up. They may derive from his interpretation of the institutional context – for instance, that he must work in order to pass examinations, or to avoid punishment.

(b) Sociological addendum

This approach seems to be one of the few issues these days which provides some common ground between philosophers and sociologists. I think it would be true to say that philosophical analyses which argue that human action is more appropriately to be understood in terms of actors' purposes, reasons and intentions than 'behavioural causes' have been parallelled by some recent sociological theorising. The tradition in sociology that man is to be viewed as actively interpreting and giving meaning to his social world has been somewhat eclipsed by the tendency of 'scientific' sociologists to conceive of man, usually implicitly, as an 'object' akin to the objects of the natural world studied by natural scientists, which responds mindlessly to the forces, pressures and conditions which allegedly constitute his social environment. However, the conception of man as active interpreter and maker of his social world, which has been kept alive by theorists such as Weber, Mead and the symbolic interactionists, and Wright Mills, has recently experienced something of a renaissance under the influence of a revived interest in 'phenomenological' sociology[29] and a more 'humanistic' interpretation of Marx. In such a view motives are not 'causal' antecedent variables (such as the dispositions to behave in certain ways inculcated by earlier socialisation), nor are they private, interior 'mainsprings of action' (such as the 'need for achievement'), but actors' purposes, intentions, reasons, justifications and accounts.

Might it not be that the pupil's motives are not formed as dispositions prior to schooling, but involve the conceptions of school knowledge which he builds up as they develop in the course of his experience through interaction with teachers and other pupils? But although, on this model, man is endowed with the possibility of choice, we must also remember that the forms of activity made available to him, from which he may choose, are not limitless: the alternatives offered to him will, to a greater or lesser degree, have been produced by other men, and therefore exist as social constraints upon his action. Hence the importance of examining, for example, the institutionally organised character of the knowledge which teachers make available in schools – a question traditionally unexamined by sociologists of education.[30] In short, the pupil must, as it were, be followed as he moves through the school, for there is evidence that in interaction with teachers and pupils within the school itself, and not simply within the home and the community, the pupil's willingness and ability to be 'educated' may be formed, maintained, modified and sometimes even transformed. However, because sociologists of education have been mainly concerned with the socialisation practices of the home, such studies as have been concerned with the school itself have not been given the prominence which in my view they deserve.

Now, I am not arguing that the early childhood experience of pupils is of no importance in trying to understand how they experience school; but I am saying that it is not necessarily all-important. Nor am I arguing that issues of social class are no longer of any significance. Rather I want to reformulate the question and ask not 'What is it in the children's background that "causes" them to fail in school?' but 'How is it that a pupil's social-class background is *made significant* in the school context by teachers and pupils?'. And what are the consequences for what the teacher does in the classroom? For is he or she knows about their social class origins he or she may have certain expectations of them which may lead to categorisation, labelling and differential treatment.

Thus teachers, by the way in which they classify and label children, having themselves helped to generate patterns of success and failure in the classroom, frequently institutionalise individual success and failure by the arrangements which they collectively make with administrators and others for the social organisation of learning in streams and schools of different status.

(c) Psychological come-back

However, I fear that I have been somewhat unfair to the psychologists by seeming to contrast their recourse to inner drives and needs with the more cognitive social approach of the sociologist with which I, as a philosopher, have much more sympathy. I have almost given the impression that most psychologists writing about motivation have been behaviourists!

It is admittedly difficult for them to say much about the cognitive variables to which I have drawn attention, because of their embarrassment about consciousness. But William McDougall about seventy years ago stressed the cognitive aspects of his instincts. Lewin and other Gestalt psychologists writing about motivation made the individual's 'life-space' central to their theories. In more recent times George Kelly, in his theory of 'personal constructs'[31] explicitly rejected any approach to motivational phenomena by reference to 'inner drives'. He started from the individual's perspective on the situation in which he is placed and the affectively tinged dimensions in which he classifies what he sees. There is then the whole realm of social psychology which is being increasingly encroached on by sociologists. Not that I am keen on demarcation disputes – but I have made it sound as if psychologists have never developed theories like these. You have only to read an influential social psychologist such as Solomon Asch[32] to appreciate how similar to my own the approach of many psychologists has been.

In the particular sphere of teaching I am not oblivious of the furore created in the past ten years by the controversial book by Rosenthal and Jacobson called *Pygmalion in the Classroom*.[33] This purported to show that favourable teacher expectations promote IQ growth. Whilst there seems to be little support for this specific hypothesis[34] it has been valuable in stimulating research into the more general influence of teachers' expectations and institutional procedures on the achievement of pupils. These can influence groups of children as well as individuals.[35] Of particular importance is the self-concept which children develop, which is very much influenced by teacher as well as parental expectations.[36] A particular example of this is the effect of streaming on pupils of low ability.[37] In a piece of large-scale research done by the NFER[38] it was found that the attitudes of teachers to streaming and their associated convictions about education are at least as important in affecting the attainments and attitudes of pupils as the grouping system actually used.

In the sphere of social control psychology teachers have relied for a long time on the work done by Lippitt and White on democratic and autocratic leadership styles and their effects on young people.[39] But, apart from the coarseness of these categories, which was soon pointed out, the applicability of these studies to classrooms is problematic. For they deal with small groups whose members performed specific tasks having clear outcomes over short time-spans. None of these properties characterises classrooms. Work later done by Kounin is a much more detailed study of techniques of control used by teachers and the conditions which affect their use such as the pupils' motivation to learn and their liking for the teacher.[40]

I could continue indefinitely with this recitation of studies. I could discourse about classroom climates, peer-group pressures, and so on.

But I am not sure of the relevance of all this to the specific issue of motivation. And that is why I have been uneasy from the beginning about my special third category of 'social aspects of motivation' except in so far as it provides a model of man which is more appropriate than the behaviouristic one of an organism stimulated by inner and outer 'drives'. For this type of evidence gives rise to the following question: given that children pick up attitudes to learning and conceptions of themselves from others, that they are imitative and responsive to social pressures and expectations, that they respond in various ways to different types of social control, why do they pick up some people's attitudes rather than those of others, why do they conform to the demands of their peers, what determines individual differences, and so on? Do we not have to postulate the operation of one or other of the forms of motivation which we have already discussed and which are pinpointed by Kagan in his contribution to *Learning about Learning*?[41] He argues that 'Developmentally the first goal is a desire for the nurturance, praise, and recognition of significant others' (p. 35). For the young child this means parents and teachers. For the older child it means peers and other authority figures as well. He then goes on: 'A second class of motives begins its growth at age 4–5 and involves the child's desire to increase his perceived similarity to a model who is (i) seen as commanding desirable resources (such as power, competence, affection) and (ii) in possession of some attributes that are also shared by the child. A third class of intrinsic motives involves the desire for competence and self-worth.' I do not want to argue about the priority of extrinsic motivation in the form of the desire for approval over intrinsic motives such as the desire to remove inconsistencies or the desire for competence. But must we not postulate the operation of some such motivation to account for imitation of some rather than others and susceptibility to social pressures? For in stressing all these social factors in motivation, there remains the problem of how they are internalised.

The psychologist is probably right about this if we are probing into ultimate explanations of a psychological sort. But from the practical point of view this more social way of looking at motivation would encourage us to pose the following sorts of questions about children who are reluctant to learn:

(i)   Instead of just theorising about the needs and interests of 'the child' we should inquire what attitudes towards learning are prevalent in the homes from which particular children come; and in the schools in which they work.

(ii) Instead of talking in general terms about conflict, discrepancy, curiosity, and the like, we should examine in detail the particular learning materials which we offer to particular types of

144/*Essays on Educators*

children in relation to their attitudes, expectations, and levels of cognitive structure.

(iii) Instead of just working on our own as teachers in the hope that we, as individuals, can change the motivation of children towards learning, we should get together with our colleagues and with the pupils themselves and examine the institutional structure of the school with special attention to the learning situation which it provides for children, its ethos and the types of incentives to learning that if offers.

(iv) We might then come to see that the problem of motivation in education is part and parcel of two wider problems:

(*a*) that of approved forms of motivation in society at large;
(*b*) that of the ways in which the school is related to society – the home, the occupational structure and other educational institutions.

REFERENCES: CHAPTER 8

1 Marx, K., *Economic and Philosophic Manuscripts of 1844* (Progress, Moscow, 1967). For recent discussion of 'alienation' see Ollman, B., *Alienation: Marx's Conception of Man in Capitalist Society* (Cambridge: Cambridge University Press, 1971).
2 For example, Holly, D., *Society, Schools and Humanity* (London: MacGibbon & Kee, 1971).
3 See Jackson, B.J., and Marsden, D., *Education and the Working Class* (Harmondsworth: Penguin, 1966).
4 See Banks, O., *The Sociology of Education* (London: Batsford, 1968), ch. 3.
5 Cannon, W.B., *The Wisdom of the Body* (New York: Norton, 1932).
6 Hull, C.L., *The Principles of Behaviour* (New York: Appleton-Century-Crofts, 1943).
7 See Weiner, B., *Theories of Motivation* (Chicago: Markham, 1972), ch. 11.
8 See Peters, R.S., *The Concept of Motivation* (London: Routledge & Kegan Paul, 1958), ch. 4.
9 Skinner, B.F., *Science and Human Behaviour* (New York: Macmillan, 1953), and *The Technology of Teaching* (New York: Appleton-Century-Crofts, 1968).
10 Zigler, E., and Kanzer, P., 'The effectiveness of two classes of verbal reinforcers on the performances of middle class and lower class children', *Journal of Personality*, no. 30 (1962).
11 Chomsky, N., review of Skinner, B.F., *Verbal Behaviour, Language*, no. 35, 1959.
12 Skinner, B.F., *Beyond Freedom and Dignity* (London: Cape, 1972).
13 Allport, G.W., *Pattern and Growth in Personality* (London: Holt, Rinehart & Winston, 1963), ch. 10.
14 Caldwell-Cook, H., *The Play-Way* (London: Heinemann, 1917).
15 For references to such theories see Millar, S., *The Psychology of Play* (Harmondsworth: Penguin, 1968).
16 Piaget, J., *Play, Dreams, and Imitation in Childhood* (London: Heinemann, 1951).
17 Herron, R.E., and Sutton-Smith, B., *Child's Play* (New York: Wiley, 1971).
18 Berlyne, D.E., *Conflict, Arousal and Curiosity* (New York: McGraw-Hill, 1961), and *Structure and Direction in Thinking* (New York: Wiley, 1965).

19 Berlyne, D.E., 'Notes on intrinsic motivation and intrinsic reward in relation to instruction', in Bruner, J.S. (ed.), *Learning about Learning* (Washington, DC: US Government Printer, 1966).
20 Piaget, J., *Six Psychological Studies* (University of London Press, London, 1968), ch. 5.
21 Peters, R.S., *The Concept of Motivation* (London: Routledge & Kegan Paul, 1958), ch. 1, and *Psychology and Ethical Development* (London: Allen & Unwin, 1974), ch. 5.
22 See also Mischel, T., 'Piaget: cognitive conflict and the motivation of thought' in Mischel, T. (ed.), *Cognitive Development and Epistemology* (New York: Academic Press, 1971).
23 See Furth, H., and Wachs, H., *Thinking Goes to School* (New York: Oxford University Press, 1974).
24 McClelland, D. C., *The Achievement Motive* (New York: Appleton-Century-Crofts, 1953).
25 Veroff, J., 'Social comparison and the development of achievement motivation', in Smith, C.P. (ed.), *Achievement Related Motives in Children* (New York: Russell Sage Foundation, 1969).
26 White, R.W., 'Competence and the psycho-sexual stages of development', in *Nebraska Symposium on Motivation* (Lincoln, Nebr.: University of Nebraska Press, 1960).
27 Banks, O., *The Sociology of Education* (London: Batsford, 1968), chs 4, 5.
28 See Ryle, G., *The Concept of Mind* (London: Hutchinson, 1949), chs 3, 4; Peters, R.S., *The Concept of Motivation* (London: Routledge & Kegan Paul, 1958); Melden, A. I., *Free Action* (London: Routledge & Kegan Paul, 1961); Kenny A., *Action, Emotion and Will* (London: Routledge & Kegan Paul, 1963).
29 See Gorbutt, D., 'The new sociology of education', *Education for Teaching*, Autumn 1972.
30 See Young, M.F.D. (ed.), *Knowledge and Control* (London: Collier Macmillan, 1971), and Pring, R., 'Knowledge out of control', *Education for Teaching*, Autumn 1972.
31 Kelly, G., *The Psychology of Personal Constructs* (New York: Norton, 1955).
32 Asch, S., *Social Psychology* (Englewood Cliffs, NJ: Prentice-Hall, 1952).
33 Rosenthal, R., and Jacobson, L., *Pygmalion in the Classroom* (New York: Holt, Rinehart & Winston, 1968).
34 See Baker, J.P., and Crist, J., 'Teacher expectancies', in Elashoff, J.D., and Snow, R.E. (eds), *Pygmalion Reconsidered* (Chicago: National Society of Study of Education, 1971).
35 See Rist, R.C., 'Student social class and teacher expectations', *Harvard Educational Review*, vol. 40, no. 3 (August 1970).
36 See McCandless, B.R., *Adolescents' Behaviour and Development* (Hinsdale, Dryden Press, Ill.: 1970).
37 Douglas, J.W.B., *The Home and the School* (London: MacGibbon & Kee, 1964), and Jackson, B., *Streaming: An Educational System in Miniature* (London: Routledge & Kegan Paul, 1964).
38 Barker-Lunn, J.C., *Streaming in the Primary School* (Slough: NFER, 1970).
39 Lippitt, R., and White, R.K.,'An experimental study of leadership and group life', in Newcomb, T.M., and Hartley, E.L., *Readings in Social Psychology* (New York: Holt, 1947).
40 Kounin, J.S., *Discipline and Group Management in Class-rooms* (New York: Holt, Rinehart & Winston, 1970).
41 Kagan, J., 'Motivational and attitudinal factors in receptivity to learning', in Bruner, J.S. (ed.), *Learning about Learning* (Washington, DC: US Government Printer, 1966).

Index